Ethnographic Interviewing for Teacher Preparation and Staff Development

A FIELD GUIDE

Ethnographic Interviewing for Teacher Preparation and Staff Development

A FIELD GUIDE

Carolyn Frank

TEACHERS COLLEGE PRESS

Teachers College, Columbia University
New York and London

Published by Teachers College Press, 1234 Amsterdam Avenue, New York, NY 10027

Library of Congress Cataloging-in-Publication Data

Frank, Carolyn.
  Ethnographic interviewing for teacher preparation and staff development: a field guide / Carolyn Frank.
    p. cm.
  Includes bibliographical references and index.
  ISBN 978-0-8077-5256-2 (pbk.)
1. Observation (Educational method) 2. Teaching—Social aspects—United
States. 3. Elementary school teachers—Training of—United States. 4. Middle
school school teachers—Training of—United States. I. Title.
  LB1027.28.F74 2011
  371.102—dc23

                                                                    2011018201

ISBN 978-0-8077-5256-2 (paper)

Printed on acid-free paper
Manufactured in the United States of America

18   17   16   15   14   13   12   11   8   7   6   5   4   3   2   1

This book is dedicated to Oscar Reese, my late father, who at 95 years old and before his death on December 1, 2010, was still building houses, riding his bicycle, attending church on Sundays, and eating lunch at the Senior Center every day. A former test pilot, airport owner, rancher, mechanic, and house builder, his main talent was his ability to fix anything, including a wire-tier clutch dog on a Minneapolis Moline baler.

Contents

Acknowledgments

I want to thank Kerri Keslow, Alison Daltroy, and Carol Dixon for reading drafts of this book and giving me suggestions for revisions. They helped to create language and ideas for the whole book and were always generous in their replies to my emails requesting their feedback.

Judith Green and her colleagues in the Santa Barbara Classroom Discourse Group provided much of the background knowledge for this book. I am indebted to this group for introducing me to ethnography and giving me a way of describing classrooms to outsiders.

Elementary and middle school teachers have always provided me with new ways of looking at children and curriculum. I am especially indebted to Lois Brandts, Carol Kamida, Ted DeVirgiles, Mary del Palacio, and the fellows of the Los Angeles Writing Project.

Finally I want to thank my students from both Cal State LA and UCSB for sharing their reports with me and for allowing me to publish them in this book.

Ethnographic Interviewing for Teacher Preparation and Staff Development

A Field Guide

CHAPTER 1

Introduction

> This is the essence of ethnography. Instead of collecting "data" about people, the ethnographer seeks to learn from people, to be taught by them. (Spradley, 1980, p. 4)

I was first introduced to ethnographic interviews when I was in graduate school at the University of California, Santa Barbara (UCSB). I took a class in qualitative research and one of our assignments was to conduct an ethnographic interview. I decided to do my interview at the Farmer Boy Restaurant, an old established restaurant in Santa Barbara, near the place I was living on State Street. As I entered, I saw booths along the right side with a row of windows above. There was a counter with stools along the left side, overlooking the area where the chefs were cooking and where the waitresses put in their orders. I sat down at the counter and became a customer. I was also a participant observer, taking fieldnotes and wondering, "What's going on here?" Every morning after, I ordered oatmeal and sat at the counter writing fieldnotes. Even though the participant observer may enter a cultural scene to watch the activities, the main question of what's going on cannot be answered until an insider's knowledge is gained. To really understand any culture, to know the insiders' perspective, the ethnographer engages in ethnographic interviews.

ETHNOGRAPHY

Ethnography is a research method used by anthropologists, sociologists, historians, and educators to study different social groups or cultures (Spradley, 1980). Ethnographers use observation and interviews to *discover* and find out new things—not always to assess or evaluate or interrogate. The people inside homes or classrooms are seen as "informants" who know about their culture and are willing to teach the ethnographer. An ethnographer who observes and interviews understands that different

1

cultures communicate in different ways. Therefore, particular homes or classrooms are understood within social and cultural contexts. Ethnographers listen to the language of the informant (the slang, the jargon) and the meaning words have to the person being interviewed. James Spradley wrote,

> Interviewing informants depends on a cluster of interpersonal skills. These include: asking questions, listening instead of talking, taking a passive rather than an assertive role, expressing verbal interest in the other person, and showing interest by eye contact and other nonverbal means. (1979, p. 46)

Insider knowledge, or observing from an *emic* perspective (observing from the perspective of those inside the culture), was reinforced for me one day when I was shopping. There was a computer-generated, 3-D picture of squiggly lines and colorful designs at an outdoor sales booth at La Cumbre Plaza, an outdoor shopping mall in Santa Barbara. If you stared at your reflection on the glass partition covering the picture long enough, and if you could train your eyes to "see" into the design, you would eventually discover a three-dimensional portrait of Bugs Bunny. When you finally found Bugs, his happy face beamed out at you as if to say, "Hey Doc, what took you so long?"

CULTURE

Although there are many definitions of *culture*, for this book I define it as a group of people who gather together regularly and over time and develop shared understandings of talk, routines, roles, relationships, responsibilities, and ways of using particular artifacts. This definition of culture would include a group of people who play chess in the park, actors who attend an acting school 2 nights a week, bridge players who belong to duplicate bridge groups, pilots who fly for Southwest Airlines, coffee drinkers who buy coffee at Starbucks, and even people who ride in elevators. By this definition, classrooms are also considered cultures (Putney & Frank, 2008).

This definition of culture includes a situated perspective, which means that the description of the elevator-rider culture would have to involve a particular elevator in a particular building at a particular time of day. The elevator riders at Dodger Stadium in Los Angeles are a different culture from the elevator riders in the Empire State Building in New York City. The culture in Miss Hancock's 2nd-grade classroom is a very different culture than Miss Soto's 2nd grade, even though they both teach at the same school. From this perspective then, people belong to many different cultural groups and as they move from one group to another, change their speech, their dress, their vocabulary, and their thinking.

An understanding of culture also includes an awareness of multiple perspectives (Green, 1992)—different vantage points, stances, or points of view. I agree with Agar (1994) when he writes, "When you run into different meanings, when you become aware of your own and work to build a bridge to the others, 'culture' is what you're up to" (p. 28). By using ethnography to understand culture, we also learn more about ourselves and how to bridge the gap between our culture and other cultures. We become more aware of other ways of being, thinking, and talking and are able to compare and contrast them with our own way. Thus, we ultimately learn more about the world and the ways of the people in it.

SCOPE OF THIS BOOK

In the chapters that follow in this book, I illustrate how ethnographic interviewing can be a useful tool for learning about classrooms, for teachers to use as a basis for cross-cultural communication with students and parents, and for classroom students to construct curriculum. I describe this ethnographic method by telling my own stories of being a teacher, graduate student, educational researcher, and teacher educator. The questions that I address in this book include (1) How do ethnographic interviews help teachers learn more about their students and parents? (2) How do ethnographic interviews help preservice teachers explore the work of their mentor teacher? and (3) How can teachers use ethnography with their students as a resource for learning more about the world?

The different kinds of interviews presented in this book include parent interviews at home, child interviews at home and at school, interviews in the native language of the child, interviews in English when the child is an English learner, teacher interviews about the child, and teacher interviews about the classroom observation.

Interviewers learn to ask questions about "typical" events. What happens during a typical day in class? What happens during a typical dinner at home? An ethnographic interviewer will take into consideration the context of the situation: Are students talking in front of other students? Are parents talking in their own homes or at school? Are teachers being interviewed over the phone or in their classrooms? According to sociolinguistics, looking at the social context of an ethnographic interview distinguishes the interview as speech events, separate from other kinds of conversations (Gumperz, 1986). In order to understand the interview in more depth, this book will examine the language use of this event in its social and cultural contexts.

DATA COLLECTION

The interviews in this book were collected from my students across the 12 years I've been teaching at California State University, Los Angeles (Cal State LA). Additional interviews are reported from when I was a doctoral student at UCSB. I received consents from all the students whose reports I have used in this book and I use pseudonyms for the names of children and parents.

My students at Cal State LA were in the Charter College of Education, learning to be elementary or middle school teachers. Most had graduated from Cal State LA with degrees in child development or liberal studies and were Latino/a American, Asian American, or Anglo American. Many were bilingual or multilingual. Cal State LA is largely a "Hispanic Serving Institution," where, in 2009, Latino students made up 46% of the undergraduate student population (Modarres, 2010). We serve the children of a working class population and most students are older, female, and Latina. Many of our students are the first to finish high school and enter college in their families.

I assigned my students a project that involved three parts. The students each had to choose a child (preferably a neighbor or relative) who would write five or six essays for them (so that the students could learn to assess writing) and whose parents would participate in a home visit. I asked my students to observe the child at school and to interview the child about his or her interests. Some students used audiotapes to record their interviews, but most just wrote down as much as they could afterward. Therefore, the interviews presented in this book are the written reports of what they remembered from their interviews and their notes. These reports are "really our own constructions of other people's constructions of what they and their compatriots are up to" (Geertz, 1973, p. 9).

Despite not having extensive experience with writing or research, my students became adept at detailing and describing the events that took place when they conducted interviews and made observations. I coached them through how to write up their reports using rich descriptions, a major principle in ethnography. Because ethnography is a descriptive science, it is dependent on the ethnographer's ability to observe and write vivid and detailed descriptions (Curry & Bloome, 1998).

Many wrote in the *ethnographic present*. This is a style of writing that is "frozen" in the present tense. It is as if writers are remembering what

FIGURE 1.1. Example of Ethnographic Interview

Carolyn: Well, you know, I'm really confused about some things. Maybe you guys can tell me as you're eating. What is this thing called rough draft? What is that?

Matt: It's like this yellow paper [goes to get yellow paper]. We go over. We take this kind of paper like white, like in our journal and then we copy it over but with capitals and periods and exclamations.

Jessica: Rough drafts is just your first try, your first writing, the first paper. When you have five done of those papers you got to tell her.

Carolyn: So when you have five rough drafts . . .

Matt: Publish it.

Carolyn: What did you say, Matt? Publish it?

Matt: You publish it.

Carolyn: What does that mean?

Matt: You fix it up. You get one of these papers [goes to get paper] and you fix it up and you do all that stuff that I just told you about [giggles] and then you publish it.

Carolyn: What does that mean to publish it?

Matt: Hm, write it. Put it in a book.

Carolyn: Can you give me an example of something that was published?

Matt: Like when you staple it. It's already dated. Like you open it up. You write on it and then you staple it and put it there.

---

happened to such an extent that they are experiencing it again in the present. The description blends with the event itself and illustrates the immediacy of what is going on.

ETHNOGRAPHIC INTERVIEWS

In an ethnographic interview, the ethnographer is the "student-child-apprentice" (Agar, 1980) who does most of the learning. Although the ethnographer may have some guesses about what the informant might say during the interview, she or he should always be ready for surprises and new interpretations of what the insider or informant might know. From this perspective the ethnographer learns to listen in order to discover information. By surrendering the outcome of the interview to the informant, the ethnographer learns to be quiet and not jump to judgments too soon. Channeling this stillness, the interviewer holds off on asking the next question until the informant has a chance to answer completely. The interviewer's goal is to make sure that all has been "milked" from the answer, using each answer as a springboard for the next question. Another important aspect of the interview is repetition, wherein the interviewer repeats what the informant has said in order to prompt filling in any details that may have been omitted. The informant must see himself or herself as the expert, as the instructor, who is trying to teach the ethnographer. Figure 1.1 gives an example of an ethnographic interview.

I was interviewing children in a 2nd-grade classroom during lunch. There were two children eating at the table inside the classroom. I wanted to know how much they knew about the terms *rough draft* and *publishing* as used during an activity at their school called writer's workshop. I learned that these 2nd-graders understood and could explain rough draft to me. They were good informants as they became experts teaching me about writing.

Ethnographic interviews are important for educators for a variety of reasons. First, thoughtful conversations between teachers and children and teachers and parents can change the relationships that teachers have with their students and with their students' families. They enable teachers to hear the insights of families and identify children's strengths—a good place to begin instruction. Second, ethnographic interviews enable teachers to learn about family practices and traditions and begin to bridge the gap between home and school.

Teachers are constantly involved in interviewing. Talking to students and parents to gain information is part of the profession. When I was teaching in elementary school, before I learned about ethnography, I often interviewed children in order to assess where they were in their development or to see if they understood a lesson I was teaching. As an ethnographer, I now understand that there is more to interviewing than just assessment. Rather than ask questions with specific answers, as I used to do, answers that I already knew, I learned through ethnography to take a broader view, to investigate more fully. I became aware of my own biases and how they were blinding me to the entire picture. I was operating as a teacher on limited information. Ethnography taught me how to step out of my own skin and look from the child's or the parent's perspective.

One of the main activities of preservice teachers is to observe classrooms and interview teachers. However, many new teachers are asked to watch events in classrooms or interview teachers without knowing how to observe or what to ask. Ethnography provides a systematic way of focusing the observation and the interview so that beginning teachers can make sense of what they see in classrooms (Frank, 1999). Additionally, interviewing through ethnography gives classroom observations and home visits more depth and enables preservice teachers to look from a broader perspective and make sense of ongoing activities.

An Ethnographic Perspective

Green and Bloome (1997) make a distinction between doing an ethnography and using an ethnographic perspective. As they write about what counts as ethnography in education, they illustrate a variety of educational studies done by teachers and students using an ethnographic perspective. Not trained anthropologists, these teachers and students defined ethnography as a language for exploring and used a set of ethnographic principles and activities in the process of inquiry. These authors argue that the use of an ethnographic perspective is useful for teachers and students as "a way of bridging the proverbial gap between theory, research, and practice that has characterized much education research" (p. 196). The preservice teachers at Cal State LA were at the beginning of their teaching careers. They had been observing classrooms and doing assessments but had very little experience with parents or individual children. Instead of teaching them ethnography, I taught my students how to interview from an ethnographic perspective. They were not really ethnographers, but for a few hours (during their observations and during their interviews) they investigated as scientists and researchers and not as teachers. Instead of doing their observations from the perspective of a teacher or student, they were asked to become anthropologists, exploring a completely strange and unfamiliar culture—the classroom. And instead of doing their interviews from the perspective of a teacher, they were asked to be curious interviewers without preconceived judgments.

An interviewer with an ethnographic perspective discovers the everyday life of the child from the child's perspective, or the homelife of the child from the parents' perspective, or the life of the classroom from a teachers' perspective (Weade & Green, 1989). Understanding how to get out of our own skin and look from a different person's perspective is not easy. When someone is accustomed to seeing life from one spot, it is difficult to understand how someone else might see the world differently. When we grow up in one culture, never being exposed to others, we think the world revolves around that culture. It is only when we see from a different vantage point that we break the cycle of rigid certainty.

Multiple Perspectives

The key to seeing life from a different perspective is understanding multiple perspectives. The concept of multiple perspectives allows the ethnographer to investigate the phenomenon of study (child, parent, homelife, classroom, teacher) from many different viewpoints. These different stances are diverse and are the only ways that we can know the

FIGURE 1.2. Steps in Conducting Ethnographic Interviews

1. Choose an informant and gain permission.
2. Write up general questions.
3. Develop rapport and put the informant at ease.
4. Explain that you want to learn from the informant.
5. Take notes during or after the interview or ask permission to make an audio recording.
6. Analyze the interview notes or transcribe the audiotape and analyze.
7. Write up the report using quotes from the informant.

whole phenomenon. For example, if the phenomenon of study is a child in our classroom, we can see the child's academic achievement by looking at standardized tests. We can interview the child and investigate their everyday work in the classroom. We can also make home visits and interview parents about the child's homelife. In this way we can know the child better and more fully in order to guide instruction.

Thick Description

To understand why description is such an important part of ethnography, I draw on the concept of *thick description*, a way of writing with many details. Ethnography is a complex descriptive science. Clifford Geertz, in his first chapter of *The Interpretation of Cultures* (1973), writes that culture is so complex and multilayered that it is only by investigating all the different parts that we truly understand it. It is as if the culture we are studying is an onion with many layers that must be peeled away one-by-one in order to see what makes up the whole. The job of the ethnographer is to describe a culture in detail: to describe each layer of the onion. Geertz tells a story that describes how ethnographic description is a never-ending story filled with many layers to be investigated:

> There is an Indian story—at least I heard it as an Indian story—about an Englishman who, having been told that the world rested on a platform which rested on the back of an elephant which rested in turn on the back of a turtle, asked (perhaps he was an ethnographer; it is the way they behave), what did the turtle rest on? Another turtle. And that turtle? "Ah, Sahib, after that it is turtles all the way down." (p. 29)

Conducting Ethnographic Interviews

Choosing an informant is the first challenge in conducting an interview (see Figure 1.2). When my students had to choose a child for the assignment, they usually decided on a neighbor or a relative. If they did not know

FIGURE 1.3. A university student interviewing a 2nd-grade student in the library at her school.

an elementary or middle school child, the task became more difficult. In that case, I gave them a number of options, including talking to a teacher at the school where they made classroom observations or linking up with an after-school program. Many of my students used LA's Best, a program to which many children go to get help with homework. This worked so well with one of my students that she ended up working with three young children who wanted to continue with her after my class was over.

The next step in interviewing from an ethnographic perspective is to gain rapport with the informant. Rapport is making the informant comfortable—making him or her realize that the interview is not an interrogation and gaining trust. (In Chapter 2, I discuss some of the ways to do this.) After gaining rapport, I asked my students to make sure the child knew that they were helping with a university assignment. If children understood that this was a favor and that they were helping my students become teachers, they were more willing to engage in writing the essays, being interviewed, and participating in home visits (Figure 1.3).

Next, my students developed questions to ask during the child interview or during the home visit. (Chapter 3 discusses questions to ask.) They took notes about the interviews and observations and then wrote them up for the report. My students did learn about multiple perspectives.

They learned how not to jump to judgments and not make assumptions (most of the time). They used ethnographic questions and interviewed from an ethnographic perspective. They made observations, conducted interviews, and made home visits. I hope, when they become teachers, they will remember these ethnographic principles and activities and use them to discover new information.

SUMMARY

In this chapter I explored how teachers might use an ethnographic perspective to interview children, parents, and other teachers. An interviewer using an ethnographic perspective understands multiple perspectives and how to use that knowledge to see from another's viewpoint. Ethnographic interviewing is useful for teachers, preservice teachers, and parents who want to educate children. By following the steps I have outlined, we may be able to see and understand the life of the child more fully. When we do that, we are able to teach the child more effectively.

Activities to Explore the Ideas

1. Choose a "cultural scene" that interests you. As you enter, pretend that you are an anthropologist studying a strange and different culture. Write down what you observe.
2. Make a list of potential informants that you want to interview from this scene. How will you gain access to them? How will you use your observations as starting points for the interview?

Suggested Readings

Frank, C. R. (1999). *Ethnographic eyes: A teacher's guide to classroom observation.* Portsmouth, NH: Heinemann.

> This is an introduction to ethnography for preservice teachers that illustrates how to record, analyze, and represent the particular kind of classroom culture that is being constructed.

Spradley, J. P. (1979). *The ethnographic interview.* New York: Harcourt Brace Jovanovich.

> This companion book to *Participant Observation* (1980) is a handbook for conducting ethnographic research with a focus on interviews. James Spradley gives specific guidelines for interviewing informants.

CHAPTER 2

Ethnographic Questions

In most forms of interviewing, questions are distinct from answers.
In ethnographic interviewing, both questions and answers must be
discovered from informants. (Spradley, 1979, pp. 83–84)

When my students were making home visits, I hesitated to give them scripted, prewritten questions that could be used with all parents all the time. Ethnographers understand that questions presuppose answers and instead try to discover the questions from the informants. When you ask a parent, "Who helps your child with his homework?" you presuppose that the child does homework at home and that there is someone who can help him. Instead of asking a question such as this, students should begin talking with the parents in such a way that hands the direction of the conversation over to the parent or to the person with the information. Parents and caretakers should see the home visit not as an interrogation from the school, but as a friendly visit from a teacher. The point of the interview is to have a conversation with parents to discover who the child is at home and where the child lives, rather than who they are at school.

Home visits by educators, however, are different from traditional ethnographic research and are not made by qualified ethnographers or even, necessarily, experienced teachers. The home visits I assigned to my Cal State LA students were being conducted by preservice teachers, just about to begin student teaching but not yet familiar with parent/teacher relationships. They were using ethnographic methods and an ethnographic perspective to interview children and parents at home. It was important to give them support.

Without guidelines for ethnographic questions, inexperienced teachers may, in the beginning, ask "teacher questions" concerning school or homework. For example, one of my students chose a child for his case study who was having discipline problems at school. When my student made his home visit, he discovered that the home was very small. One of the first questions he asked the father was how many people lived in the home. He asked him about his educational background and how that influenced the child's education. He also wondered where the child would do homework, and when asked, the father told him that the child did it outside. As with this student, without realizing it, inexperienced interviewers can ask questions that may be considered offensive, such as "teacher questions" about homework or TV watching. Figure 2.1 gives guidelines for developing ethnographic questions.

My students were more successful when using the guidelines I gave them as jumping-off points for a friendly conversation with the child or the parents. Home visits should be a friendly visit from someone who wants to know more about the child.

ETHNOGRAPHIC INTERVIEWS AS SPEECH EVENTS

Ethnographic interviews can be seen as "speech events" (Agar, 1994). Different forms of speech demand different discourses or different ways of talking. I explain this to my students by suggesting some different contexts in which people communicate with each other in different ways. For example, a job interview is different from a book club conversation. A conversation at a rock concert among friends is different from a lecture on music in college. A sales pitch from a car salesman can be compared with the opening act of a late-night entertainment show to demonstrate the differences in speech events. Different events require different modes of communication or different ways of talking.

A speech event can be identified by the kind of talk going on. It can be broken into different parts or elements. A friendly conversation might begin with a greeting and then continue with turn taking, each participant adding something to the conversation. This kind of speech event has no explicit purpose but is flexible in nature. People in friendly conversations usually try to avoid repeating themselves and use abbreviations since both parties know each other (Spradley, 1979). For example, when you meet a friend on the street, you might first greet them and ask how he or she is doing. The friend might talk about a vacation he or she is taking, and then you might talk about a trip you recently took. If you include names of people, the friend would not need you to explain who they were because the friend would already know.

An ethnographic interview is different from a friendly conversation. In the first place, the two people may be strangers and rarely are topics abbreviated. Topics have to be explained in detail. These interviews do not usually contain the back and forth, give and take of turn taking. Since the ethnographer's goal is to elicit information, the conversation usually begins with a long introduction about what the ethnographer wants to

FIGURE 2.1. Guidelines for Developing Questions

1. *Introduce yourself.* Teachers making home visits might begin with a long description of themselves, why they are making the visit, and how the parents can help by sharing what they know about their child.
2. *Be open-minded.* Although the ethnographer may have some guesses about what the informant might say during the interview, s/he is always ready for surprises and new interpretations of what the insider might know.
3. *Learn to listen.* The ethnographer learns to listen in order to discover information from the informant. By surrendering the outcome of the interview to the informant, the ethnographer learns to be quiet and not jump to judgments too soon. With this stillness comes an attitude of holding off on asking the next question until the informant has a chance to answer completely.
4. *See the informant as the expert.* The informants must see themselves as the experts, as instructors who are trying to teach the ethnographer. The interviewer must convey this to the informant.
5. *Don't interrogate.* An ethnographic interview is a conversation between someone who wants to know and someone who knows. Conversation and language are at the heart of understanding how to interview. There is a difference between a friendly conversation and an interrogation.
6. *Build rapport.* The ethnographic interview is a friendly conversation between two people who may not know each other very well. Knowing how to begin, when to interrupt, when to be quiet, and how to end are important considerations. Putting the informant at ease and letting them be the guide is critical in order to learn as much as possible.

know and how the informant possesses all the knowledge. For example, when Spradley (1979) interviewed a cocktail waitress at Brady's Bar, he recorded how he began the interview:

> *Ethnographer*: Well, let me explain what I'm interested in. I would like to find out what it's like to work as a waitress. I guess what I want to know is if I got a job at Brady's Bar and worked there for a year or two, how would I see things? What would I have to know to do a good job and survive and make sense out of what goes on? I'd like to know what you do each night, the problems you have, just everything that goes into being a cocktail waitress. (p. 62)

There is quite a bit of repeating on the part of the ethnographic interviewer and it is important to avoid abbreviating. An interview I did with an artist in Santa Barbara illustrates the use of repetition: I repeated some of the answers she had given me during an interview the previous day. I did this in order to understand the vocabulary of this particular artist and to get exact meanings for her words:

> *Carolyn*: You said, "Sometimes a single painting will lead to a series." How does that work?
>
> *Artist*: Well, I get an idea for a painting and I'll do it and then I'll ask myself, "What other way can I do this idea? How can I explore this idea in more depth?" Just like the variations on the theme of the black icon. What other fragments of landscape can I use and what other things can I add on besides screws and nails. Game pieces. I have one with dominoes, chess pieces. Variations on a theme. Exploring an idea until you push it and push it so you exhaust it. (Cynthia Martin, artist, personal communication, May, 1995)

GRAND TOUR QUESTIONS

The main kinds of question for an ethnographer are descriptive questions known as "grand tour questions" (Spradley, 1979). Asking these questions is a way of getting the big picture or a way of providing a lens into other people's experiences. Spradley breaks apart these questions into domains such as space, time, events, people, activities, and objects. For example, an ethnographer interviewing a teacher and using a grand tour question about space might ask, "Could you describe all the different areas in your room?" I used these same domains with students in education and translated them into questions that my students could use with children and parents (Figure 2.2).

Having guidelines does not mean that students will not encounter problems. Inexperienced preservice teachers may struggle with how to use grand tour questions with parents, children, and other teachers. For example, Catherine chose a child who was a recent immigrant from China and whose parents spoke Mandarin. Since Catherine also spoke Mandarin, she translated one of the ethnographic questions ("Could you describe the main things that happen during the month, beginning in September and going through May or June?"). Catherine reported that she struggled trying to translate this question into Mandarin and eventually had to go on to another question since the mother was confused. Questions such as this need to be changed by the interviewer when confusion arises. Rather than leaving the question, an experienced interviewer would revise the question to fit the circumstance. For example, the interviewer might ask, "What are some of the things you do with the family during the whole year?"

FIGURE 2.2. Questions for Ethnographic Interviewing

The main kinds of questions for an ethnographer are descriptive questions such as *grand tour questions*. By asking these questions the ethnographer can get the big picture. A parent might give a teacher that is making a home visit a grand tour of the home. Or a preservice teacher might ask the master teacher some of these questions during a grand tour of the classroom. There are a variety of questions with which one could begin this grand tour:

About space. Could you describe your home to me? (Or ask the child to describe his/her room.) Could you describe your classroom to me?

About time. Could you describe the main things that happen during the month, beginning in September and going through May or June? Could you describe what happens during the first day of school?

About events. Can you tell me all the things that happen during dinner? Could you describe a typical day in your classroom? Can you tell me all the things that happen in a reading group?

About people. Can you tell me about friends and relatives of your child? Can you tell me the names of all the office staff and what each person is like?

About goals. What are all the things that your child is trying to accomplish? What are your goals during writing workshop?

About objects. Could you describe some of the objects in your child's room? Could you describe all the math manipulatives in the class?

Developed from Spradley, 1979

The overall question for an ethnographer is, "What's going on here?" Preservice teachers engaging in ethnography want to know what is going on with the children they work with. They want a fuller picture of each child's life, including the homelife. An ethnographic interview is a conversation between someone who wants to know and someone who knows.

Conversation and language are at the heart of understanding how to interview. There is a difference between a friendly conversation and an interrogation. The ethnographic interview is a friendly conversation between two people who may not know each other very well. Knowing how to begin, when to interrupt, when to be quiet, and how to end are important considerations.

Questions About Space

Spradley (1980) writes that there are nine features or dimensions to every social situation. *Space*, or *place*, is just one of those features. When forming grand tour questions, the ethnographer sees each of these features as guides to asking questions during an interview. For example, one preservice teacher, Jenny, was successful in getting the mother of a child to describe her home, her space, in detail. In this case, the interview led to a story about the home and how the mother cooked in it, how she felt her home was a comfortable place to raise a family, and how she was living "the American dream." Because of this question about space, the informant did most of the talking, an important characteristic of an ethnographic interview.

> Well, I live in a four-bedroom-and-one-bathroom apartment. One bedroom belongs to me and my husband, one belongs to my son, and the other two bedrooms belong to my daughters. There is a large kitchen, which is like heaven to me. I enjoy cooking very much and I always make a lot of different foods like beans and rice, chicken, tacos, fajitas, tamales, burritos, and lots, lots more. It is an apartment building so we do not have a backyard to plant things like fruits and vegetables. We have a small bathroom and a large living room. We have TV and a big living room with soft sofas. There are many books on the shelves and pictures hanging on the walls too. Everywhere there are toys because of my kids playing with them and all over. They never put it back. We lived here for about 10 years when we emigrated from Mexico and I love this place. The neighbors are nice and the weather is beautiful. The community is safe for the kids and, especially, this home is very cozy and comfortable. The big windows let the sun shine through the glass and bring a lot of natural sunlight into the room. The high ceilings make the place look bigger and the colors of the walls are light blue because [sic] it feels like we are in the sky or at a beach. It is very relaxing for us. Ahh . . . This is *mi casa*, my house, where I born [sic] my children and raise them. To help teach them what is right and wrong and making sure they have good manners. I feel like I live in the American dream because I have kids that are healthy, a great husband who works hard, and *mi casa es muy terrifico*! In other words, my home is very terrific. *Mi casa*, where I welcome people with open arms and say, *"Ay, mi casa es su casa, mi amigos."* It means "Ay, my home is your home, my friends." (Jenny)

Questions About Time

Another feature or dimension of a social situation is *time*, or the sequencing that takes place over time. For example, a teacher making a home visit might ask the parents, "Could you describe the main things that happen during the month, beginning in September and going through May or June?" This question is difficult but if the parent understands and is willing to comment, it gives students lots of information. The following answer was from a mother of a 2nd-grade English learner who was at first hesitant to allow the home visit. It was only after the child kept insisting that my student was a "kind and nice individual" that they decided to help with this assignment. The mother's native language was Spanish and my student was a Chinese American who spoke no Spanish:

> I remember we go to church events like the fair every weekend of every month and we go help out at the homeless shelter. We went to Las Vegas at summer vacation but just on the weekend to attend a family wedding. We mostly stayed home and spend time together reading books like our Bible or go walk at the park. I take the kids to the playground and get them ice cream when the days are hot. I go [to the] market to buy food and cook for family barbeque where relatives and friends come to eat and we all spend time together. I get busy watching my three kids and watch me [*sic*] telenovelas on the TV and listen to my *musica* en *español* like mariachi band. (Jennifer)

Another answer to questions about time came from one of my students who was a Spanish speaker and was interviewing a mom who also spoke Spanish. The child was a 5th-grade English learner.

> My first question was, "What is a typical day like at home from Monday through Friday, which are school days for the child?" The mother told me that the child wakes up at 6:30 a.m., makes her bed, leaves her room clean, goes to school to eat breakfast at 7:00 a.m., stays after school in LA's Best, and gets picked up at 5:30 p.m. Her homework is completed during LA's Best so when the child gets home she has the evening free. As I was at their home I got to observe, meet, and find out that 11 people live with my child. This includes the child, the child's parents, the child's younger brother, an aunt with her four children plus a child that she has guardianship of, and a cousin of the mother that moved in. (Marisela)

Questions About Events

Another dimension of social situations is *events*, or the related activities that people carry out. For example, when interviewing a child, the teacher might ask, "Can you tell me all the things you do during recess or lunch?" Some questions about the events in the homelife ("Can you tell me all the things that happen during dinner?") seem to evoke common patterns. For example, two of my students received very similar answers to this question:

> She informed me that she always tries to have everyone at the table for dinner. She considers it very important and refers to it as "special family time." At the kitchen table, they spend time talking about their day, about school, and or any other miscellaneous items of conversation of that day. (Nelly)

> Dinner *es muy importante*. It is where we all sit down at seven o'clock, *exactamente*, and pray to God for being thankful to have food on the table, clothes on our backs, and shelter to live in. We talk about what we did during the day and I ask my husband how the *trabajo* was like and the kids how school was like for them. We would all sit down and share our stories of our lives. (Jenny)

Other features of social situations include *people, objects, goals,* and *feelings*. These dimensions help interviewers develop questions, and the answers give a more complete picture of the child or the homelife of the child.

Side Stories

Side stories, or vignettes, that don't seem to be on topic often come out of other grand tour questions. They are the detailed stories of our life that illustrate more completely who we are and what we do. For example, LA's Best is an after-school homework program instituted in various schools in Los Angeles. Because Los Angeles has such a large immigrant population, many children's parents find it difficult to help with homework, which is in English. The next interview illustrates how frustrating it is for parents whose native language is not English. The student doing the interview was bilingual in English and Spanish:

> One of the things that I was interested in learning was a typical day for Liliana on a day-to-day basis. Her mom began to explain to me that in the mornings it is difficult to get Liliana and her younger brother to wake up in the morning and there have been times when Liliana has been late to class. Since she gets off work a little after Liliana gets off school she stays in the after-school program until she comes to pick her up. She expects Liliana to have done her homework in the program although she confessed that that's never

the case. She feels overwhelmed because since she doesn't speak proficient English she is unable to help Liliana with her homework. While she was cooking *arroz con pollo* (chicken with rice), she mentioned instances where Liliana has gone up to her asking her for help and she couldn't read the directions that were in English. I explained to her that when I was younger I had gone through a similar situation with my parents, but that they did the best they could in helping me so that she shouldn't be too hard on herself. (Katey)

Two things are of interest in this interview. First, my student spoke the same language as the parent. This always seemed to engender more rapport with the parents. Immediate trust seemed to appear. The story that the mother tells reminds my student of similar circumstances in her own life. She is able to respond back to the mother with words of encouragement, making this interview more of a friendly conversation than an investigative interview. Second, the mother talked to my student while preparing a meal (*arroz con pollo*). Talking over food seemed to be one of the magic ingredients in getting parents to talk about their children.

ELEMENTS OF ETHNOGRAPHIC INTERVIEWS

An ethnographic interview has different parts including beginning the interview, developing rapport or putting the informant at ease so that they can guide the interview, asking questions, and ending the interview.

Beginning the Interview

Teachers making a home visit might begin with a long description of themselves, why they are making the visit, and how the parents can help by sharing what they know about their child that the teacher might not know. For example, one of my students began talking to the mother of her child with a long description of herself and why she was doing this interview. The beginning of the interview is the most important since it is then that you convince the parents that you are not there to interrogate them or talk about school. This long introduction should tell the parents about yourself and who you are and why you are there. Amy began with this introduction:

Once everyone was seated, I introduced myself and explained the project I was doing. I could tell at first that they were nervous about why I was there. So I decided to try to make them feel more comfortable. One of Daniela's topics for writing was about her vacation to Mexico during the summer. I told them that Daniela had mentioned that they were all in Mexico last summer and I told them that my husband and I visited some of his family in Mexico City the year before. It was amazing to see the change in her parents by mentioning that one fact. Her mom said, "Oh, your husband is Mexican," and proceeded to talk more excitedly about their family. By the end of the interview they invited my husband and me to come to their son Jose's baptism party. (Amy)

Another preservice teacher, Angelica, began with this introduction that helped the parents know her better:

I began my ethnographic work by talking about the detour I had to take in order to get to their house. Then I introduced myself officially to both James and his mother. I explained that I am a student at Cal State LA working on the credential program to become an elementary school teacher. I also explained where I am from, where I live, and how I know the family member who referred James to me. (Angelica)

Having official documents to back up the interview is also a good strategy. Nelly began this way:

The first thing I did was thank Isabel for her time and for allowing me to visit and observe her son. I showed her all of my class paperwork, such as the official observation forms, my syllabus assignment, and my ethnography questions just so she can get a better idea of what I would be working on with her son. I also verbally explained in detail what the assignment entailed. (Nelly)

The beginning of the interview is critical. Teachers might want to take along official documentation and be prepared to talk about themselves as a way of a friendly introduction.

Putting Parents at Ease

Part of the interview with the parents includes making them feel at ease. Home visits are not common and many parents have never experienced having a teacher come to their home. Parents are as nervous as the students. Putting them at ease, in order to learn as much as possible about the child, is part of the interview. My students used innovative and creative ways to do this. For example, one student was given the remote to the TV and made everyone laugh when he turned to a soap opera. Another talked about getting lost on her way to the home. But often it was the language that helped to ease the first introduction. If my student spoke the same language as the child's parents, an immediate connection was made and the interview seemed to create more information. For instance, in the next example, putting the parents at ease was easier when my student spoke Spanish:

Sergio, the child I am observing, lives in the area of Hollywood very close to downtown Los Angeles. As I drove up to his home I was a little nervous, since I really did not know what to expect. When I arrived at his apartment building I dialed his number on the intercom and a woman answered the call in Spanish. She said, "*Bueno, quien habla* (Hello, who is calling?)" I told her that I was from Franklin Elementary School and she said oh yes come up to apartment number 55. As I walked up the stairs to the apartment building I saw Sergio run out of his apartment and say, "Ms. Jimenez, you're here!" He then led me into his apartment. When I walked into Sergio's home, there were his parents sitting on the couch. I immediately introduced myself in Spanish and thanked them for letting me come into their home. They spoke to me only in Spanish and told me to have a seat. Sergio's mom offered me something to drink. Sergio sat next to me as I sipped on water they gave me. I whispered to him, "Can you introduce me to the rest of your family?" He said OK and walked to the kitchen and said, "This is my grandma. She cooks for us every day and this is my little sister. Her name is Esmeralda. She is 5 years old." I then noticed a family picture above the dining room table and asked Sergio's mom who were those people in the picture. She said that it was a picture of all their family in El Salvador about 2 years ago. I said, "Oh really. I'm from El Salvador too." When I told them that, they were very interested in knowing more about where my parents grew up. I told them all the details about what I knew of El Salvador and the family that lived there. (Sandy)

Gaining Trust

An anthropologist living with a community for many years and participating in the social activities will usually acquire the trust of the members. For preservice and student teachers doing ethnographic interviews, it can be much more difficult to gain trust based on only one visit. However, if a student is successful in creating rapport with the parents, and if they are successful in asking questions that prove they want to know more about the child and not just interrogate the parents about homework, then they can be successful in discovering information about the child. In this next example, my student learned during an interview with the child that she and her brothers had been adopted. Therefore, during the home visit, my student asked about adoption:

Viviana's mom was very candid and willing to talk about [Viviana]. One thing I asked about was the fact that Viviana and her two older brothers had all been adopted by Clara and her husband. The child mentioned it during our talk, but I was interested in getting more information. Clara told me the whole story. She and her husband were not able to have children. Her husband saw a segment on a Spanish talk show about Hispanic adoptions. They filled out paperwork and went through interview after interview. When the social worker told Clara about the three siblings, she was nervous. She thought they'd get one, maybe two. They didn't want the siblings separated. Clara is one of six children and couldn't bear the thought of the three of them being torn apart. It was hard at first, she said, but they became a strong family. When Viviana was 5, there was a surprise: Clara was pregnant! Now she has four children and life is busy, but she wouldn't have it any other way. (Stephanie)

Because the child had first mentioned the adoption to Stephanie, she felt that the topic could be mentioned to the parent. Also, because Stephanie felt that "trust," or a confidence between two people, had been gained, she believed she could ask about the adoption.

Marisela was another student who gained the trust of the parent. In this case, she spoke the same language as the parent, a condition that may have made a difference:

The mom told me how she truly believes education is very important for her daughter. I agreed with her and she continued by telling me her story of how she brought her daughter to the United States from Mexico when she was only 4 years old. She told me how she did not have the same opportunity that her daughter has experienced in school. The mom only reached 1st grade. Therefore, she has put a great value on education so that her daughter can continue valuing it and getting the most out of it. I agreed with her and told her how my parents went through the same experience as they both only went up to 2nd grade. Therefore, they have also taught me to value education and strive for the best. She then told me something that I was surprised about, but I thought it was brave of her to share it with me. She told me she cannot read or write and how it is something that she is ashamed of and does not want her daughter to go through. (Marisela)

Because Marisela shared her own story with the mom, about her parents only reaching 2nd grade, she gained enough trust with the mom so that the mom felt confident to share that she was illiterate. We gain the trust of informants by sharing our own stories with them, by explaining to them the purpose of the visit and the need to know more about the child. We gain rapport with an open attitude and a sense of wanting to know rather than judging or evaluating. If interviewers want to understand, they must not interrogate but, rather, ask respectful questions that demonstrate a willingness to see from the informant's perspective.

Ethnographic interviews are more complicated than traditional interviews. The different parts are intended to put the informant at ease and help them understand that they are the one giving the information. Another part is putting the informant at ease, or breaking the ice. Finally, trust, or rapport, must be developed between the informant and interviewer or the information gained will not be trustworthy.

FOOD AS A SOURCE OF CULTURE AWARENESS

In every culture the preparation and presentation of food provides a window into the actions, beliefs, and characteristics of that particular culture (Spradley & McCurdy, 1972). The things people eat, the way the food is prepared, and the people who prepare the food are different in all cultures.

As my students entered the homes of the children, they were offered a variety of dishes by generous parents. It was a way of welcoming my students into their homes. But it also helped to foster cultural awareness in my students. Food and how it is offered is a good illustration of the culture of the family. It often tells more about how the family lives than does an answer to a direct question. If you are offered *caldillo*, knafeh, or spring rolls during a home visit, you have the chance to experience food different from your own culture.

If my student spoke the same language as the child's parents, they were usually not surprised with the offering. For example, one of my students who spoke Spanish reported, "I was asked to stay for dinner and I gladly accepted. I ate beans, rice, salad, and a dish they called '*Caldillo*,' which is a mixture of potatoes and ground beef. The food was simple, yet so satisfying" (Sarah).

Another example came from a student who was Lebanese American. She chose her nephew for the case study and when she was offered something to eat, she was familiar with the food:

> The parents' culture is very much so part of Masoud's life. The food is Middle Eastern in nature including the tabouli and baklava. The guest at their house is greeted warmly and offered Turkish coffee first and then sweets. This time I was offered knafeh. This is a typical Lebanese dessert that Masoud's mother made from scratch. (Rana)

Comparing cultures was second nature to my bilingual students, who lived their homelives in one culture and their academic lives in another, and many thrived on making comparisons between cultures when it came to the food. Francisco (perhaps over-generalizing) made a distinction between "American culture" and "Latin culture" when he visited his child's home:

> I was expecting to be offered a full plate of food because of the culture. Often, when I visit my American friends, I am offered a glass of water or soda. In Latin culture, however, a full plate of food is a common offering. Moments later, I was offered a plate of steak, rice, and beans. I accepted and entered the kitchen to begin eating. (Francisco)

On the other hand, if my student had chosen a child whose language they did not speak (as was the case almost always with English-only students), then eating a meal at the home was a different cultural experience. One such student chose a 9-year-old Vietnamese American child:

> Chi asked me to take my shoes off. As soon as I entered I noticed a giant Buddha statue. In the living room, they had the largest fish tank I have ever seen in a home. There were carved wood Vietnamese people framed on the wall and paintings of Vietnam. There were two large plates of food on the large coffee table in front of the couch in the living room. The mom asked me to sit on the couch and have a bite to eat. One of the plates was all sliced fruit. The other plate was full of random food including spring rolls with a dipping sauce, which was delicious. Mom told me that Chi loved

pho, which is noodles with sliced beef, and *bun rieu*, which is a
tomato-based soup with shrimp and cooked tofu. Chi's favorite food
was chicken nuggets from McDonald's. (Vanessa)

Although the children came from homes where the foods were very
different, it seemed that the favorite of many was chicken nuggets!

Family Stories

The questions that educators ask during home visits will likely bring
out actions, beliefs, and perspectives from parents that are deeply rooted
in past experience. Family stories or narratives help students understand
parent perspectives. James Gee writes that "one of the primary ways—
probably the primary way—human beings make sense of their experience
is by casting it in a narrative form" (1985, p. 11). Mishler (1986) asserts
that one of the advantages of ethnographic interviewing over traditional
survey interviewing is that stories from informants are more likely to create meaning between the interviewer and the informant. Mishler writes:

> We are more likely to find stories reported in studies using relatively
> unstructured interviews where respondents are invited to speak in
> their own voices, allowed to control the introduction and flow of
> topics, and encouraged to extend their responses. (p. 69)

One of my students, Kyoung, was Korean American and chose a
Korean child who was looked after by the grandfather. Kyoung and the
grandfather became good friends and talked often about his own stories
(Figure 2.3). Kyoung's report on her home visit with Hana highlighted
what she learned from Hana's grandfather:

> Hana's grandfather is from Korea. He is 78 years old. He has been
> in the United States for about 20 years. He enjoys talking about
> his life and is pleased to answer any questions I have for him.
> I spoke to him in Korean. He grew up when Korea was under
> Japanese occupation. He was forced to speak only Japanese in
> school. The Korean language was forbidden. Like many people
> of his generation, he can still speak basic Japanese. Life was hard
> under Japanese occupation. They did not respect the Korean people
> and wanted to tear down the culture. After Korean War in 1950,
> the grandfather's job was a clerk in a department that controlled
> rationing. Goods were still in very short supply. He often had to go
> to the ports to look at cargo in connection with his job. In the ports,

FIGURE 2.3. Hana's grandfather. Many caretakers are able to tell family stories, which adds richness and detail to the cultural background of our students.

he would see Korean children asking American soldiers, "Give me chocolate." These were the only English words the children knew. The U.S. soldiers were kind and generous. The grandfather thought that after Korea's independence from Japan in 1945, Korea would be free and life would be good. Things did not work out that way. In 1950, the war began between South Korea and North Korea, and life remained difficult. "We were unlucky," he said. People of his generation always speak about the Korean War. Before he came to live in the United States, he had often visited. He had several cousins living here. Sometimes he had stayed for several weeks. Twenty years ago, he decided he could make more money in the United States. He and his wife left Korea for Los Angeles. He and other family members worked for a garment factory. It was a good business, he said, even though he had a lot of competition from other countries. He told me that sometimes he gets homesick. But he has many family members here, and they make him happy. He is very helpful to his granddaughter and walks with her and her younger brother to school every day. He makes sure she concentrates on her studies. He feels a special responsibility to her because her father spends most of his time in Seoul. The father has a good job working for the Korean government. The grandfather, his wife, Hana, and Hana's younger brother and mother all live together in an apartment. As a leader of the family, he tries to be a father figure for the family. (Kyoung)

One of the advantages of ethnographic interviews compared to survey interviews is that answers are in the form of stories, as seen in Kyoung's experience with Hana's grandfather. Because there is more time to talk, informants often will tell about their lives in narrative fashion. These stories give much more context and meaning than answers to yes or no questions. Because the informants are answering questions in their own surroundings, they will often feel more secure in sharing life stories. And if the teacher has been successful in gaining rapport and developing trust, parents will often have longer conversations, narrate experiences, and give teachers more information about children.

This is not to suggest that narrative responses to answers are the only valuable kind. Choosing to highlight family stories, and choosing to see ethnographic interviews as a way of eliciting family stories, however, is a productive way for teachers to gain meaning and understanding about the lives of children.

In the interview that Kyoung conducted with Hana's grandfather, Kyoung first asked questions from the ones I suggested in class (Figure 2.2). She asked about "things that the child's teacher might not know." But after these questions were over, Kyoung and the grandfather talked for 2 hours. She wrote, "It was a delightful time for me to talk with the grandfather. He is almost 80 years old and enjoyed telling me about his life story. He said he hoped to talk to me again" (Kyoung).

Ethnographic interviews take time. After questions are asked and answered, there is time for eating or for telling family stories or listening to side stories. These vignettes add richness and detail to the culture and life of the child. It is only through these details that we can truly understand and teach.

SUMMARY

Understanding the ethnographic interview as a particular kind of speech event (Agar, 1994) enables the interviewer to use certain techniques to elicit information. In this chapter I have explained the different kinds of questions used in ethnographic interviews and the elements of an interview. Examples from home visits illustrated that ethnographic interviews were successful in getting parents to talk more about their children and offering student teachers many family stories from different cultures.

Activities to Explore the Ideas

1. Review the examples given of various kinds of descriptive questions and prepare several types for informants in the cultural scene you are studying.
2. Conduct and record an ethnographic interview with an informant using descriptive questions.

Suggested Readings

Agar, M. (1980). *The professional stranger: An informal introduction to ethnography.* New York: Academic Press.

Describing many of his experiences along the way, Michael Agar shows readers how to conduct ethnographic research from the perspective of a linguistic anthropologist.

Spradley, J. P. (1980). *Participant observation.* San Francisco: Holt, Rinehart & Winston.

One of the two primary texts used by qualitative research doctoral students, this book details how to conduct ethnographic research from a cultural anthropological perspective.

CHAPTER 3

Interviewing Parents During Home Visits

The difference with this program is that teachers get a chance to listen. We ask questions about the children, such as "What does your child like to do?" or "What are your hopes and dreams for your child?" It makes a difference to me as a teacher to visit students at home and hold their baby sister, see where students do their homework and meet their grandparents. (David Fisher, as quoted in Posnick-Goodwin, 2007)

Home visits by elementary school teachers are not new. Experienced, exemplary teachers have engaged in them for many years. I first heard about home visits from a teacher in Santa Barbara, Lois Brandts, who allowed me access to her classroom for the 2 years I spent researching writing workshop (Atwell, 1987) for my dissertation. An accomplished storyteller, Lois knew the power of conversation when teaching children. The words she spoke conveyed to her students what she taught them all year: Be kind to your peers, learn to notice things around you so you can write about them, read books with your friends, appreciate art, and learn to be storytellers. While making home visits, Lois encountered Mike, a child who was being considered for special education:

I am blown away by my visit to Mike's house. One of the old farms tucked back where you can't see it. Great spacious old place with gracious and wonderful old and new stuff to look at and do. They raise orchids in a HUGE greenhouse and Mike is an absolute expert. He has wonderful places to play and hide and be an outdoors kid. He was so polite and thrilled that I was there, made me some guacamole from their own avocado trees, gave me avocados, an orchid, and a copy of a Monet that he and his big sister did. He is a bit lonely except when he has cousins/friends over. Does that explain his socializing nature at school? We are going to take the kids on a field trip to his place and you have to go and film. You won't believe it! Susan thinks that he might be headed for resource. Hell, I think Mike is going to be just fine . . . with or without the reading expertise. What a wonderful little human being he is. I suspected it all along, now I know it. I learned remarkable things and was kicking myself for not going earlier. (Brandts, personal communication, spring 1997)

Other teachers also use home visits as a way to learn more about children's lives outside of school. Teachers in Sacramento participate in the Parent/Teacher Home Visit Project, a partnership between the Sacramento City Unified School District and Sacramento Area Congregations Together. The project differs from the traditional parent/teacher conference in that teachers go to the child's home instead of the parent coming to the school. It also differs because the teachers are trained to approach the home visit in a nontraditional way. Usually, when a teacher calls home, the conversation is about attendance or behavior problems or homework. In this project, teachers are taught how to listen instead of talk and ask questions such as "What does your child like to do?" and "What are your hopes and dreams for your child?" (Posnick-Goodwin, 2007).

To be successful, teachers need to know as much about their students as possible. Learning about the whole child is not possible if the teacher only knows the child at school. Children at school are different from children at home, and parents are different at school than they are in their own homes. Teachers therefore cannot know the whole child until they learn more about the child's life at home. For example, one of my students wrote about how she learned the value of a home visit in order to construct a more complete understanding of the student she worked with and not jump to judgment based on limited data:

Visiting Maria's home was an extraordinary experience that helped me learn about her, not only as a student but as a person as well. I learned about this student's likes and dislikes as well as events in her life that may affect her performance in the classroom. It was very important that I did not jump to labeling this student as being isolated and timid since I did not have enough background information about her. After speaking to the student, her teacher, and parent, I realized that Maria is a very outgoing child that enjoys doing many of the activities that other kids her age enjoy. The fact that she was eating alone during lunch and that she would not interact with her classmates was due to the fact that she was a new student in the classroom and was still adapting to a new environment. This activity taught me that I should not label students based on their behavior in the classroom. Instead, I should take the time to learn more about them on an individual basis. (Ariana)

Many preservice teachers are surprised when they learn the importance of home visits. The Sacramento Parent/Teacher Home Visit Project is a good illustration of how home visits are beneficial, increasing parent involvement, improving student achievement, improving attitudes toward school, and improving classroom behavior (Posnick-Goodwin, 2002, 2007). Another example of the value of home visits is exemplified by the experience of a 41-year-old White, monolingual student teacher living in an affluent community north of the university. Aurora had reservations about joining the teacher education program at UCSB because, at that time, there was a special focus on bilingual education and she wasn't bilingual. Her first assignment was in a bilingual 6th-grade classroom. One of the teacher education assignments was to draw a neighborhood map (describe the neighborhood where children in her classroom lived) and four of Aurora's students volunteered to walk her around the neighborhood. When she was invited into the home of one of her students, she explained how she felt:

> My senses are overwhelmed. I smell great aromas coming from the stovetop, see too many people in a small area, and feel conspicuously like I'll be perceived as "checking them out." There's a part of me that wants to look around at everything I can, but the other part of me is telling me that would be disrespectful. I thought I could learn about their culture by just having them in my classroom, but I now realize that when they're in the classroom, they're experiencing my culture, not theirs. (Aurora, as quoted in Frank, 1999, p. 20)

This was a difficult assignment for Aurora, but after she did it, she was able to see from a different perspective. She was able to see that the classroom may offer very different cultural experiences from the ones at home. She appreciated knowing more about her students and understanding what life was like in their homes. As she wrote, she was crossing over into another person's culture:

> As we're walking, one more student joins us. I am told that another student and her family have a Mexican candy store so I suggest we go by there. We head for the candy store and I'm in for the next lesson of this educational walk. The "candy store" is actually "M's" living room in a small apartment complex. There are an incredible amount of people there, children and adults, not to mention a couple of more students from our class!! I am so stunned to realize that they are selling this candy, etc. from their living

room. I am invited in and told that I can pick something for free! I just want to stand there and take this incredible experience in. This is like something I have never encountered and that's because I am now experiencing someone else's culture. (Aurora, as quoted in Frank, 1999, p. 20)

ETHNOGRAPHIC INTERVIEWS DURING HOME VISITS

An ethnographic interview between a preservice teacher and a parent during a home visit is different from a traditional ethnographic interview. An ethnographer lives within the community he or she is studying for many years. Doing an ethnography of less than 1 year is not considered a true ethnography in academic circles. In contrast, a preservice teacher using ethnographic techniques and doing an interview from an ethnographic perspective is only with the family for a brief time, perhaps only 1 hour. However, the goal in each case is the same—gaining rapport and eliciting information.

The ethnographic interview during a home visit is a special kind of speech event. As I discussed in Chapter 1, my students making home visits were not anthropologists using ethnography but, instead, were using an ethnographic perspective to interview parents during home visits.

Gaining Entry and Gaining Access

Two of the most important and difficult problems for an ethnographer are to "gain entry" to the site where the informant can be interviewed and then "gain access" to the informant. When I did ethnographic research at the Farmer Boy Restaurant in Santa Barbara, gaining entry was not difficult since I entered as a customer. Eventually, I was able to gain access to an informant by convincing the manager to let me interview the waitress, Norma. However, depending on the culture that is being studied, gaining either entry or access may be a challenge. For example, one ethnographer tells the story of what happened when he wanted to investigate a funeral home:

> One Sunday afternoon as I started to enter a large mausoleum, a camera dangling from my neck, wearing sunglasses and an old pair of jeans, my hair hung in wisps over my coat collar, I sauntered into this plush carpeted mausoleum. The crystal chandeliers sparkled and in the distant background soothing music floated through the halls to comfort the bereaved. And a voice challenged, "Where are you going?" In a self-confident tone I answered, "I'm just looking around." I continued down the hall. "Where do you think you are going, you'd better come back here." "Can't I just look

around?" I asked. "No, you can not," he said. "Why not?" "Because you weren't invited." (Schroedl, as quoted in Spradley & McCurdy, 1972, p. 178)

Gaining entry for my students also presented challenges. Because preservice and student teachers do not yet have a classroom, it is more difficult to contact a child and the parents. To overcome these challenges, on the first night of class, we discussed the kind of child they would choose for the ethnographic interview assignment. First, the child had to be able to write essays for my student since the course was on how to assess student writing. Therefore, children in grades 4 through 8 would be ideal to work with. Second, students were required to observe the child at school. Third, they would interview the child. Finally, and most importantly, the assignment included a home visit.

As a preservice teacher making the first foray into home visits, it can be helpful to select a participant with whom entry and access are already established. There are a number of ways to do this, such as through a neighbor or relative, a class the preservice teacher observes, or through an after-school program.

If a student chooses a child who is a neighbor or relative, then the family is the one to give them access (to the child and to the home) because the student usually knows the neighbor or the relative and trust has already been established. However, if a student decides to work with a child from the school where they work, then the child will be the one to provide access to the home. Selecting a student to work with from an after-school center is the most difficult option, because it involves gaining entry to the teacher in the after-school center and then proving credibility as a preservice teacher doing a legitimate assignment for a university. Figure 3.1 is an example of a letter I gave my students at Cal State LA to boost their credibility.

Another way of finding a child is to ask a mentor teacher. Such was the case with the next example:

The hardest part of the home visit was actually working up the nerve to tell the teacher that I needed to meet with Annie's mother and/or father, in their home, as part of my project. I had this horrible image of her laughing and saying something akin to "Oh, we don't do that!" Of course I was wrong and the teacher was very helpful and passed along the message. Annie's mother called me rather quickly and was very receptive to a home visit. (Monique)

When my students finally agreed to conduct the visit, it changed their whole outlook on teaching in elementary and middle school. They came

FIGURE 3.1. Letter to Parents and Teachers

To Parents and Teachers:

Students in my class at Cal State LA (EDEL 416—Writing Instruction) are
on their way to becoming elementary and middle school teachers. One of
the assignments for my course is the Literacy Assessment, which will enable
teachers to assess the writing skills of second to eighth graders. Students are
asked to choose an intermediate-grade student (an English Language Learner) to
observe, assess, and instruct. After observing the student in a variety of contexts
and events, interviewing the student and the teacher, and conducting a home
visit, students collect a variety of writing samples. They interact with the child
and conduct writing conferences. Be assured that the students' names will be
kept confidential and will be removed from their papers.

We fully expect this to be an enjoyable experience for you and your children.
If you have any questions or problems, please don't hesitate to call me.
Sincerely,

Dr. Carolyn R. Frank
California State University, Los Angeles
cfrank@calstatela.edu

---

back with wonderful stories of how the families welcomed them into the
home and the beautiful meals they were served. They were amazed at the
proud looks on the faces of these children who loved having "teacher" in
their home. One of my students reported:

> The girls were so excited to have the teacher at the house. They kept
> coming up to me to show me pictures, their room, their favorite
> toys, movies, and of course asking a lot of questions of me. They
> ended up ordering pizza and I stayed and had dinner with them.
> Overall, it was a great experience. I had to admit that I was nervous
> and wasn't sure if I could go through with it, but I did. And I noticed
> that after that visit both the child and the parents became more
> responsive towards me. In other words, they go out of their way
> to say hello, send notes, and they also invited me to their birthday
> party. I felt it helped build a better home-school relationship
> and opened the communication between the parents and me.
> (Elizabeth)

I encouraged my students to choose neighbors or relatives for their
first home visits, in part, to maintain a level of safety. It is important to
remember to be careful when and where you go, and it may be a good
idea to go with a partner during the daytime.

Two points about access need to be made. When you gain access, you don't have it forever. It constantly changes and evolves and can even be lost. Gaining access to an informant carries responsibilities. For example, I recently visited an elementary school in Alhambra, California. A teacher came up to me and told me she was in my class 8 years ago. She said that she was still in contact with the child she chose for the ethnographic interview assignment. The child's homelife was not stable but she and the child had kept in contact and now the child was in high school and doing well. Although my students had a different kind of access, the personal relationships built through gaining access, as in Elizabeth's case, still remained.

Developing Rapport

Rapport, or trust, between the informant and the interviewer develops over time. There are a number of stages to this process, including apprehension, exploration, cooperation, and finally participation (Spradley, 1979). For example, when I first interviewed Lois, a 2nd-grade teacher in Santa Barbara, I was shocked that she spent the whole time talking about her students. Over time I learned that Lois was constantly teaching me, and if I listened well she would show me that, for her, it was all about the children. She would say later, "The kids don't march to the center very often."

Once my students gained access to the home, their job was to develop rapport with the parents and try to make them comfortable with the visit. The students created various ways to do this and I offered other ideas (Figure 3.2).

One student described this as the "ice-breaking period" and was able to help the parents get over their nervousness. He was bilingual in English and Spanish and was interviewing a child whose parents spoke Spanish at home:

> When I knocked on the door, Sofia's older sister answered right away as if they were watching me walk up their front steps. I was told to have a seat on their couch and then offered the remote control to the television. Her dad told me to feel free to change the channel to what I wanted to watch. I was impressed. So to break the ice, I changed the channel to Telemundo and said, "Is it okay if I wait for Marichuy to come on?" Marichuy is the main character on "Cuidado Con El Angel," a telenovela or Spanish soap opera. We all burst into laughter because in Latin cultures only the women in the house watch Spanish soap operas. It is acceptable for a man to

FIGURE 3.2. Rapport-Building Strategies

Rapport refers to a harmonious relationship between ethnographer and informant. It means that a basic sense of trust has developed that allows for the free flow of information (Spradley, 1979, p. 78).

- Pay attention to friendly relationships within the culture you are studying.
- Listen and observe how relationships are built within the group and let that be your guide.
- Think of "ice-breakers" to reduce the stress at the beginning of the interview. For example, you might talk about your drive to the interview or you might share the documents for the interview.
- Explain in detail what the home visit assignment entails: that you want the informant to teach you, that you want to know about the child from their point of view, that you want them to do most of the talking.
- To help reduce the apprehension at the beginning of the interview, use descriptive questions to get the informant talking and keep them talking.
- Make repeated explanations of what you want, restate what the informant says, and be nonjudgmental in your responses.
- Once the informant understands that they will be teaching you, cooperation and participation lead to more detailed information.

---

watch these shows but they are often not considered too masculine. So when I said this, it was exactly opposite of my appearance, thus making it a joke. (Francisco)

AGAINST A THEORY OF CULTURAL DEPRIVATION

Describing the home is one of the first things that students report when conducting home visits. Before I illustrate some of my students' descriptions, it is important to remember that these students were using an ethnographic perspective and they were learning the principles of ethnography as they engaged in home visits for the first time. Before they started, I taught them about the problem of "jumping to judgment" when doing ethnographic observations in classrooms (Frank, 1999). When we judge or evaluate something and base our interpretations on incomplete data, we sometimes miss what is really going on. And if we rely on our preconceptions, we tend not to hear what is being said.

My students were adept at describing the home they were visiting without making assumptions about the people living inside because they understood that differences in culture do not translate to differences in values. The theory of cultural deprivation is a controversial idea that arose in the 1960s to explain the educational failure of children, their lack of achievement in school as a result of "cultural deprivation." This theory has been largely debunked by scholars and the academic community. From a different perspective, Spradley (1979) describes how ethnography gives a more complex answer when looking at the everyday lives of children:

> However, ethnographic research on the cultures of "culturally deprived children" reveals a different story. They have elaborate, sophisticated, and adaptive cultures which are simply different from the ones espoused by the educational system. Although still supported in some quarters, this theory is culture-bound. Cultural deprivation is merely a way of saying that people are deprived of "my culture." (p. 11)

GRAND TOURS OF THE HOME

As you recall from Chapter 2, *grand tour questions* are meant to get the informant talking about their experiences and can be asked about specific places, typical events, or people. Grand tour questions during a home visit can begin by asking the parent to describe their home or to describe the objects in the child's bedroom (see Figure 2.2).

Asking parents to tour the home was a popular request by my students. One student visited a father who lived alone with his son in a trailer:

> Jorge's father gave me a grand tour of his home. He lives in a trailer that contains a kitchen with a sink, a refrigerator, a bar/dining area with granite countertops and two bar stools, a 42-inch television with Direct TV, a futon bed used as a sofa throughout the day and a bed at night, and a restroom with a stand-up shower, toilet, and sink. In addition they have a few pets found inside. They have a cat, a lizard in a terrarium, and a fish tank containing three goldfish. Outside the trailer, they have a patio with a table that seats four people, a few trees, and a 20-inch television. When I asked the father to describe his home, he replied, "It's comfortable, small but cute and the right size for us, Jorge and me." He then smiled and laughed. (Luz)

Not all my students observed in low-income homes. Vanessa found herself in an "upscale neighborhood":

> Chi lives in Diamond Bar in an upscale neighborhood. I had to call the home to enter a gate to even enter the neighborhood. I really

was not expecting Chi to live in such a wealthy neighborhood. When I drove up to the house it was a large, new, and extremely nice home. (Vanessa)

However, this was unusual. Most of my students lived and worked near Cal State LA and chose children from schools near our university. Since I had asked my students to choose English learners, many of these children were from families who had recently immigrated. In some situations, many family members lived in houses with only one or two bedrooms. Poor conditions do not always breed discomfort, however, and home visits can help illuminate that point. For example, in one case, my student found that even though the parents lived in small quarters with many relatives, the homelife was "quite impressive and admirable":

I visited Angel's home on a Friday night and was I in for a new experience. He lives in the La Puente area and most of his neighborhood has Hispanic families. He lives in a house with his parents, three siblings, two grandparents, two aunts, and two uncles. In total there are twelve people living in a two-bedroom house. It was quite full of people but everyone seemed to be in good spirits and get along well. I entered the house and was immediately received with a hug from Mom and a handshake by Dad. They welcomed me and told me to feel right at home. I have to admit I was a little surprised at how welcoming they were to someone they had only met once before. Using the tips from the ethnographic questions I opened the conversation by asking them to describe their home to me. It was interesting to notice that they did not immediately address the physical look of their home, but rather began talking about the people living in it. It was nice to know that the most important part of their home was the people that live there. Mom mentioned that at dinnertime, if just one person is missing, the table seems empty. I found that interesting and kind of funny seeing as how at my dinner table every night, it is just my husband and me. Their family dynamic is quite impressive and admirable. (Sarah)

ELICITING INFORMATION: OBSERVING THE HOME

Home visits are important for teachers when we realize how the homelife affects school. The most effective classrooms are those in which the teacher and parents work together. Most of the students at Cal State LA were bilingual and some were multilingual, and many lived in urban areas. Some came from very poor circumstances. Still, they were often surprised at the living conditions of the children they interviewed. For instance, Susan was a multilingual preservice teacher taking my course. During her home visit, she learned about the dangerous circumstances of urban children walking to and from school:

> Her aunt picked us up at the front door of the tutoring center, which sits on Jefferson Avenue, a main street with constant, high-speed traffic. The four children, her aunt, and I walked a few yards down the street as the children talked loudly. Suddenly, her aunt yelled for everyone to dart across the street. So we all ran haphazardly across four lanes of traffic with the headlights of oncoming cars bearing down upon us. This is their normal routine. (Susan)

While elementary and middle schools may be safe havens for children, the urban areas where they live are filled with unexpected experiences. Getting to and from school may be a concern for some children. Susan continued to describe the apartment where the child lived:

> The apartment building is on Jefferson Avenue, adjacent to a narrow, dark alley. We entered through an unlocked metal gate and arrived at their front door. Their apartment was lit warmly, and I casually greeted her father, who was sitting on a couch just a few feet from the door with her younger brother in his lap. The older sister, who speaks a little English, introduced me as the *"maestra"* and I shook the father's hand and he offered his name. As far as I could tell, the entire apartment is roughly the size of our classroom (15′X15′). It is orderly. However, I could tell the apartment is old and not well maintained. The tiny living room contains two small couches and a very large television, which occupies an entire wall. On the other wall, pictures of the child and her siblings are hung. In all, the child's mother, father, three siblings, and herself live in that apartment. (Susan)

Many students working in urban communities may find the same kind of environment when they make home visits. Children in low-income and recent immigrant communities face specific challenges when it comes to education. Homework, learning English, and academic standards take on a whole new perspective when viewed from the parents' eyes. Library books, having a place to do homework, and supplies like paper and pencil become important issues in certain situations. Many parents find that the after-school centers are the only places where someone is able to help their children with the English homework. Three examples from my students were typical of most of the reports of home visits:

I learned that Susan lives with her older brother, two older sisters, mom, dad, and grandparents. She is the youngest in the family. Some of the activities that she participates in during the weekend include piano lessons, swim classes, religious school, watching TV, playing with her six little cousins, and going to church. When I asked her to describe some of the objects in her room, she explained that she did not have a room to herself because there is not enough room for her to have her own. She said that she shares a room with her parents and there are two beds, a bookshelf, and a statue of Virgin Mary in their room. (Annie)

The child lives there with her two sisters, parents, aunt, and one other lady. The child's bedroom was a small room with bunk beds. I asked the child who slept in the room with her and she said that her two sisters [do] and her parents as well. The parents slept on the floor and the three girls shared the bunk beds. The mom then told me that the aunt and the other woman that lived with them shared the other room. (Maritza)

As I arrived at the apartment complex on San Gabriel Blvd, I saw Chunhua playing in her apartment lobby with her siblings. Chunhua then directed me to her own apartment, which was very small with one bedroom. Chunhua showed me how she sleeps on the couch that is set up in the living room. She then showed me how her parents, brother, and sister share the one bedroom that they have. (Basma)

One of the most important reasons why I ask my students to engage in home visits is to show them how beneficial it is for the children. It is an exciting adventure to have the teacher come to your home. It is also one of the best ways for the teacher to discover the interests of the child. Having children or parents fill out interest surveys is much different from discovering what children love to do at home. Visiting the home and discovering more about the child's homelife is a good way to begin teaching. When the teacher knows the interests of the child, she or he can provide academic resources (reading and writing materials) to guide instruction. (See Chapter 4 for more on this.)

In this next home visit, my student was already familiar with the mother and the child. Trust had already been established and so it was easier for my student to learn about the interests of the child. The child was developing a list of topics to write about and wanted to add another topic to her list on her American Doll closet in her room, and so she took my student upstairs to her room:

Neon green walls and a bright pink shag area rug are the first things that you notice in her bedroom. After adjusting your eyes, you realize her bedroom is typical of an 8-year-old: twin size bed, books on the bookshelf, and toys that include her American Dolls, her prize possessions. They are stored in her American Doll closet— made by her father, who is a wood worker in his spare time—that is really a 2' x 5' cabinet. She has three dolls, five outfits, and six pairs of shoes. When asked which doll she liked the most, she said, "The one that looks like me." I asked her which outfit she liked the most, and her answer surprised me. It was not the one with the frilly dress, or colorful skirt. It was the one with the black pants and white t-shirt, and she happily proclaimed, "I wore an outfit like this yesterday." (Audrey)

Audrey's report of this child's room and Basma's report of the room where Chunhua sleeps are good illustrations of the importance of teachers knowing the culture of the home. How does the information elicited from these two preservice teachers inform the classroom teacher about the students? These two little girls bring entirely different perspectives and resources to the classroom, and that certainly impacts their academic abilities.

SUCCESSES AND PROBLEMS WITH HOME VISITS

There are challenges when conducting home visits. However, the benefits of making a visit outweigh the problems. The information learned about children at school is just that—children at school. It is only one piece of the puzzle. To know the whole child, elementary teachers need information from parental perspectives, and need to know where the child lives. Typical comments from my students after they finished the home visit included:

I did really enjoy the assignment even though at first I was extremely cautious. I liked the inside look at where children live and collecting information from parents of things that teachers may not know. Overall my experience was positive and I did really enjoy the food and the hospitality of the family. (Vanessa)

It is very interesting how much the children are mentioned, especially their immersion in the culture at the levels of behavior and beliefs. It is intriguing to watch how much the home influences a child at school. (Rana)

This experience really allowed me to learn more about Chunhua from her mother's perspective and I became aware of all the responsibilities that she has to take care of once she gets home before she starts her homework. (Basma)

Home visits can be a difficult assignment for students. Most have never encountered this kind of project, being more used to reading textbooks and writing academic reports than driving to different parts of a city and speaking to parents. A few of the students, who could not get permission or who were too nervous, took an alternative I offered and investigated the neighborhood instead of going into the home. Some principals are unfamiliar with home visits and may want confirmation from the district offices before allowing them. One principal in the Los Angeles area said that the legal department in the district would not allow home visits because once a dog had bitten a teacher and the district was afraid of being sued. Therefore, unless you are the classroom teacher, it is important to select who you work with carefully and, as stated earlier, it is often easier to work with children who are neighbors or relatives. For example, one of my students wrote about selecting a neighbor to work with:

For this assignment I not only wanted to choose a student who would benefit from the methods and strategies I have learned from this course, but one who seemed interesting to me, raised thought-provoking questions, and made me examine my own thinking concerning the writing process. The student I choose is a neighbor of mine who moved to Temple City from China in 2003. I will refer to her as Lili. Lili is a 10-year-old 4th-grader at Jones Elementary School. I choose her because she is fairly new to this area and is an ESL student. Although Lili's first language is Chinese, she has had the opportunity to learn and speak English during her last 3 years of school. Living across the street from her has helped me monitor her writing process and has made the home and school visits very easy and comfortable. (Diane)

Home visits can also be stressful at the beginning for students. One of my students wrote about her tension before meeting the parents:

On October 14, 2009, it was a cold Wednesday morning. Just like any other day, I gathered my materials and started making my way to the Gomezes' house. My stomach was turning into knots and I gripped my steering wheel with hands of nervousness. My heart was beating so fast that I felt like it was going to burst out of my chest. As I was driving quietly and endlessly, thoughts were popping into my head as to how should I conduct the interview. How will it go? What will take place? While the questions came running in and out of my head, I snapped back to reality and saw that I was already nearby her area. At last, I made that final left turn and I drove up a little hill. As I was searching, looking, and browsing for the child's beige Spanish style looking apartment building, I noticed that the community and/or neighborhood were surrounded by luscious, green berry bushes and tall, beautiful trees that smelled of pine. It turns out that she actually lives nearby the elementary school, which was within walking distance. I looked at the number of the houses and there it was: 555. I parked my car and then walked up the steps and knocked on the door. As it was thrust wide open, right away, the family greeted me with open arms and big bear hugs. (Jenny)

WHEN THE TEACHER DOES NOT SPEAK THE LANGUAGE

Interviewing in English will be the typical experience for many teachers who attempt ethnographic interviews or home visits. What happens when the teacher does not speak the same language as the child or the parents? There are a number of different strategies teachers can use to address this. Having the child as the interpreter during the home visit seems to work well. These bilingual children are familiar with this role and probably learn some things by doing it. Bringing a translator from school is another possibility, although the scheduling for this can be difficult.

If neither of these options is available, I think the home visit is still possible. While talking to parents is an important aspect of the home visit, another part is to observe where the child lives and under what circumstances they are able to do schoolwork at home. What are the resources available? If English is not spoken, then the teacher knows that help with homework is needed. Observing the home gives teachers a wealth of information about the interests of the child. Knowing information such as that one student likes science and math and that others know about video games gives preservice teachers more resources for guiding the instruction and meeting the needs of each child.

FIGURE 3.3. Protocol for Ethnographic Interviewing of an Adult (to be used during home visits)

Task: Interview parents during home visit

Time Frame: One hour

Setting: Inside the parents' home

Data Collection Methods: Head notes (writing down everything after the interview)

Purpose:

- To interview parents
- To understand the homelife of a child
- To learn about the child from the parents' perspective

Interview Questions:

1. Would you describe your home to me? Would you describe your child's room?
2. What happens in your home during a typical weekday? What happens on the weekends? Can you tell me all the things that happen during dinner?
3. Can you tell me the special talents that your child has? What does your child like to do? Does s/he have friends in the neighborhood?
4. Can you tell me what favorite foods your child likes to eat?
5. What do you know about your child that I would not know about him/her at school?

SUMMARY

Teachers use home visits as a way of learning more about children's lives outside of school. Knowing how to use ethnographic questions during a home visit gives the teacher a way of gaining as much knowledge as possible. This chapter illustrates that home visits are possible and that not only experienced but novice teachers as well are capable of engaging parents in conversations in their homes. Such topics as gaining entry, developing rapport, and taking grand tours of the home were discussed.

Activities to Explore the Ideas

1. Find an after-school homework center in your area. Try to gain entry and then go through the steps of gaining access, developing rapport, and eliciting information.
2. Interview the person in charge of the center. See if you can use your knowledge of ethnographic interviewing and go through the same steps you used in the first activity.

3. Try making a home visit with a relative or neighbor. If you are a teacher with a classroom, conduct a home visit with one of your students. (See the protocol in Figure 3.3 for guidance.)

Suggested Readings

Agar, M. (1994). *Language shock: Understanding the culture of conversation*. New York: William Morrow.

Professor Agar reveals how deeply our language and cultural values intertwine to define who we are and how we relate to one another.

Spradley, J. P., & McCurdy, D. W. (1972). *The cultural experience: Ethnography in complex society*. Prospect Heights, IL: Waveland Press.

This book has examples of short ethnographies from students of Professor Spradley and Professor McCurdy in an introductory anthropology class.

CHAPTER 4

Interviewing Children

Ethnographers who insist on visiting and studying children from the rigid perspective of adulthood will in the end understand the reality of childhood no better than tourists who visit another land and do their best to bring their "home" along with them. (Tammivaara & Enright, 1986, p. 234)

In this chapter I discuss how to engage in ethnographic interviews with children. My first experience interviewing children was at the University of California, Santa Barbara, during a class on qualitative research. One of our assignments was to conduct an ethnographic interview. I chose Karen, a 1st-grade child, thinking I would find out what books she liked to read and why. If possible, I hoped to use the advice given by Tammivaara and Enright (1986) in their article on interviewing children, which focuses on the relational aspects of interviewing.

As a former 1st-grade teacher and a mother of two children, I knew it was going to be a challenge to let go of my authoritarian position with this 1st grader. I was going to have to give the child a reason to talk to me other than my being an authority figure. I wanted to try some ethnographic techniques like "playing dumb," repeating information, and being silent. I wanted to let the child tell me how things made sense to her, what it was like reading books from her perspective. I was an experienced teacher interviewer but this time I wanted to be an ethnographic interviewer.

To prepare for my interview, I devised an interview protocol to use as a guide, illustrated here in Figure 4.1, which is one that an ethnographer interviewing an adult might design. Tammivaara and Enright tell us that not controlling the context, playing dumb, and engaging children in activities while interviewing is important. So I revised my protocol to reflect their advice. Figure 4.2 shows an interview protocol designed for use with children, which is one that an ethnographer interviewing a child might design.

Difficulties arise when an ethnographer desires information from children. These difficulties stem from the fact that the adult belongs to

FIGURE 4.1. Teacher Interviewing a Child: Protocol #1 (developed before reading Tammivaara & Enright)

Task: Interview a child in 1st grade

Time Frame: 20 minutes

Setting: Inside a 1st-grade classroom

Data Collection Methods: Audio recording and fieldnotes

Purpose:

- To develop an interview protocol for use in later research
- To practice interviewing a child inside a classroom
- To understand classroom life from the child's perspective

Interview Questions:

1. Could you tell me what happens in this classroom during a typical day? If I were a new student in this classroom what could you tell me about this classroom? What do you do in the morning? Afternoon?
2. If you were the teacher in this classroom, what would be some of the things you would be doing? What kinds of things do the children do?
3. Can you read me part of a favorite book of yours? (Or if the child is unable to read) Can you pretend read? Can you tell me the story without reading the words?

---

only one of the dual worlds of children. If the ethnographer wants to discover what life is like for the child in the child's environment, from the child's point of view, then the researcher must step out of the adult world and somehow connect with children on their level. Tammivaara and Enright (1986) see this as an issue of adult control "because of the inherent power/authority position that adults typically hold over children" (p. 229). The authors describe challenges when interviewing children having to do with context (where the interview is held) and language (in what language the interview is conducted).

CHALLENGES WITH INTERVIEWING CHILDREN

Giving Up Control

When conducting ethnographic interviews, the ethnographer must always consider the relationship between themselves and the informant. Control is one part of that relationship. With children, the issue of control is magnified. When the ethnographer is trying to discover the life/world

FIGURE 4.2. Teacher Interviewing a Child: Protocol #2 (developed after reading Tammivaara & Enright)

Task: Interview a child in 1st grade

Time Frame: 20 minutes

Setting: Inside a 1st-grade classroom

Data Collection Methods: Audio recording and fieldnotes

Purpose:

- To develop an interview protocol for use in later research
- To practice interviewing a child inside a classroom
- To understand classroom life from the child's perspective

Interview Guidelines:

1. *Don't control the context.* Control of both the physical context and the context of the conversation must be given up by the adult and given over to the child. (Could I do that?)
2. *Don't ask questions.* Since children associate questions with lessons, the researcher must forget about interviewing in the traditional sense and instead think of it as a moment-by-moment experience. The ethnographer does not want to be thought of as "just another teacher." (I look so much like a teacher. How could I change my appearance?)
3. *Play dumb.* Asking "negative valence" (Goody, 1978) or dumb questions may be a good strategy. (For example, I could use a picture book as an interaction device and start to read it backwards. Would the child then "show" me how to read it correctly?)
4. *Setting.* The interview should take place in a natural setting and therefore should be done inside the classroom. The timing of the interview will be important and should be conducted as part of an ongoing activity such as free reading time.
5. *Engage the child in activity.* Have the child draw a map, for instance.

of the child from the child's perspective, it is important to give up as much of this "control" as possible. This can be accomplished in two ways. First, the ethnographer must explain at the beginning of the interaction that the child is to be the teacher. "Playing dumb" works well with children and it can be fun when the adult pretends they do not know. In this case, the adult really does not know and must convince the child that this is so.

Second, the child should be given as much choice as possible. This means that the child chooses when and where to do the interview. There will be limits on the types of questions asked, but if the goal is to learn about the child, their interests and experiences, then the questions are not as important as the answers. The goal with children is to make it as unofficial and informal as possible and have the interview be spontaneous, fluid, and open.

Corsaro (1981) points out that two behaviors by ethnographers must be avoided when interviewing children. The first is controlling the actions of the child during the interview. Telling a child where to sit, how long to talk, how not to behave—to stop fidgeting or stop being silly—will only increase hesitancy in the mind of the child and remind them that the adult is in control. This is often difficult for adults, and in one instance that Tammivaara and Enright cite, after a 4-year-old informant selected a quiet pillow corner to play and talk in, the child promptly snuggled up and fell asleep (Tammivaara & Enright, 1986).

The second behavior to be avoided is doing all the initiating within the interview. If the goal is to understand the culture of the child, then the child must guide the ethnographer. Specific questions within a certain time period will only emphasize to the child that the interview is really a classroom lesson and not a way of understanding life from the child's perspective.

There are other reasons why children are hesitant to talk about themselves or their interests during an interview. It can be culturally insensitive to talk about yourself and seen as rude. It can be that no teacher has interviewed the child before so that it comes as a surprise when the teacher wants to know about him or her. It can also be strange because children might not think adults will understand or appreciate what interests them.

Language

Understanding and appreciating the language of the child being interviewed is important. Cook-Gumperz and Gumperz (1981) discuss children's transition from oral language to written language. Child language from these researchers' perspective is viewed as an entirely different kind of language from adult language rather than as developmentally immature. They argue that in Western cultures, child language has traditionally been seen as preadult language, as an undeveloped form of the language. It is viewed as an apprenticeship to adult language. These authors offer another view from other cultures, which understand child language as distinctly different from adult language and originating from other sources. Ashanti, a West African people, exclude young children from birthing rooms, where women are giving birth, because they think an infant would talk to the baby in the womb in the special language they share and warn it of the difficulties of life. The baby would then be reluctant to emerge, thereby causing a difficult birth. In other words, the Ashanti perspective illustrates that we may not give sufficient importance to the transition from child language to adult language. Hence, we dismiss the knowledge of young children and think of them as underdeveloped instead of realizing that their language is culturally different from our adult language.

Tammivaara and Enright (1986, p. 227) present one event during a research study that demonstrates how difficult it is to interview child informants who create their own vocabulary and language usages.

[Scene: It is "booktime" in a bilingual (Spanish/English) kindergarten classroom. The students are sitting or sprawling on a large rug, with the teacher doing household tasks in the background. Two boys, Tomas (5 years, 3 months) and Manuel (6 years, 2 months), huddle together sharing a single picture book, which they are examining page by page and talking about together. The following is a segment of their conversation.]

Tomas: This is a monster. I like all of this book.

Manuel: Look it. Look at *ella, puede mover la cola y se la corta!* (Look it. Look at her, she can move her tail and chop it off!) [Refers to two dinosaurs in the book. They turn the page.]

Tomas: I don't know that one, you take it.

Manuel: *Te la doy.* (I give it to you.) [They turn the page.] *Ya! Ese es mio!* (This is mine.) [He slaps the page.]

Tomas: No, wait, it, wait! *Los dos ganan al cabo!* (The two win at the end!) [They turn the page.]

Manuel: [As he slaps the page] Oh—blooyea! *Blooyea eso!* (Blooyea this one!)

Tomas: Blooyea. [Said softly as he takes his hand up from on top of Manuel's, who had slapped the page first. They turn the page.]

Manuel and Tomas: [Simultaneously] Blooyea! [Both slap the page.]

Manuel: Blooyea to this one! [They turn the page.] *Nos pasamos uno, pasamos este* (We skip one, we skip this one.) Okay.

Tomas: Uh-uh [negative].

Manuel: Uh-huh [positive]. *Porque sabes que?* (Because you know why?)

Tomas: Remember [get louder], blooyea that you say? Remember? [They turn the page.]

[The discussion continues for approximately 5 minutes, with discussion of the pictures in the book and intermittent slaps on pages and "blooyeas." After the activity is terminated by the teacher and the boys head for a table, the Investigator talks with Manuel.]

Inves: Manuel, come here, I want to ask you something!
Manuel: [Coming up] What?
Inves: Did you like that book?
Manuel: Yeah!
Inves: You guys kept saying "blooyea" while you were reading it.
    What does "blooyea" mean?
Manuel: [Eagerly] I don't know! What?

The question by the investigator assumed that the word "blooyea" held some meaning for the children, that the boys shared this unknown meaning, and that they were capable of explaining that meaning to an outsider. When we examine the lives of children, making assumptions from our perspective as adults does not offer the best results. This is magnified when we look at the lives of second-language children. Instead, the ethnographic interviewer must not ask for meaning but must ask for use.

Spradley (1979) writes that during the beginning stages of an interview the informant explores what the ethnographer really wants. What does he or she want me to say? Can the person be trusted? Am I answering questions as I should? Does he or she really want to know what I know? To offset such doubts, Spradley suggests asking questions about how the language is used. Perhaps if the investigator had "played dumb" and role-played reading a book with Manuel, the meaning of "blooyea" could have been realized. Manuel and Tomas could have been taken to the rug again with the investigator and the scene could have been reenacted and questions could have been asked about how the boys would use "blooyea."

CASE STUDY: INTERVIEWING KAREN

During my first ethnographic interview with Karen, the 1st grader, I would have preferred to let her choose the physical context for our interview. However, I was confined by the classroom and she had to come to my special little space away from the other activities (which kept getting her attention). As will be seen with many of my students at Cal State LA, when they were able to interview the child on the playground or the library or even the home, the interview was more successful.

During the first half of the interview with Karen, she was polite, quiet, and timid and she waited for me to direct the conversation. I quickly realized I couldn't probe for a certain kind of information, such as her favorite book. With the power relationship being the way it was, I was not going to discover her life from her point of view. In order to do that, I had

FIGURE 4.3. Map of Lunch Tray: Engaging the Child in Activity. I asked
Karen to draw a map of her lunch tray and as she drew and explained
the different parts, I wrote what she said.

"And this is where
we put our straws
and our spoons."

"This is where
we put the hot
dog or the pizza."

"That's the big
outside of the
tray."

"This is
where I
put my
milk."

"And
my
napkin."

6/1/94 child's map of lunch tray
drawn during interview inside classroom.

to suspend my "adult-centrism" and discover the child's world from the
child's point of view. I needed to suspend my adult perspectives, supposi-
tions, attitudes, and values. I had to hand over control and stop initiating
the questions.

Therefore, during the second half of the interview, when I stopped
initiating the questions and we started talking about lunch, Karen's voice
became louder and more natural. She spoke to me as one would while
having a conversation with a peer. Now we were discussing a topic that
the child knew more about than I did and she controlled the content
of the conversation (see Figure 4.3, Map of Lunch Tray). As the expert,
she could confidently describe the lunch procedure to me without thinking I might correct her. During the lunchroom conversation, Karen and

I maintained a fairly neutral relationship and she was able to give me a glimpse of life in 1st grade during lunchtime.

Although the interviewer often has specific questions in mind such as the child's favorite activity or understanding of a lesson, it is important to limit direct questioning and follow the interview in the direction the child takes it. This is a problematic aspect of interviewing children because what we want to know is discovered by questioning but questioning is not recommended when trying to uncover the child's perspective. Instead, probing the child informant for more detail often leads to a wealth of information.

Two types of probes that work especially well for children are silent probes and repeating probes. If I remained silent, then Karen would usually expand on a topic. For example, when she started talking about pizza:

> *Carolyn*: Did the pizza come from Pizza Hut or did the school make it?
> *Karen*: Sometimes we get this place's pizza but I don't like that kind.
> [I became silent and waited.]
> *Karen*: And see those tables over there. There're usually more and when they're out and when it's lunch time, all of them are out on the patio and that's where we eat our lunch. And they use garbage cans, and we dump our pizza there.

Instead of using specific, directed questions with her, I also used repeating probes. A repeating probe is executed when the interviewer repeats something that is said. This is a strategy that works well with children. For example, I said to Karen, "You said you might be talking about where you would be meeting?" This brought out the information that before children leave the lunch tables, they must raise their hand to be excused and then get "waved good-bye" by the "yard duty." When we were discussing what the children talked about at lunch, I repeated something she had previously said:

> *Carolyn*: So you talk to Nicole about meeting?
> *Karen*: Yeah, like see, pretend that we're sitting next to each other and she just got waved good-bye. Before she would leave, I would say meet me at the big toy or meet me at the grass or something like that.

I could now ask her what she meant by "got waved good-bye" (the lunchroom aide would excuse them if they raised their hands) and "the big toy" (a large piece of playground equipment). Learning the language of the informant ("got waved good-bye" and "the big toy") is critical to the ethnographer in order to understand the cultural perspective and to be able to communicate in their language.

PRESERVICE TEACHERS INTERVIEWING CHILDREN

Every quarter my students at Cal State LA have an assignment for which they must choose a child who is an English learner and who can write five or six essays that they will assess. The assignment also includes observing the child at school, interviewing the child, and making a home visit with the child's parents. The interview is intended to be a friendly conversation through which my students first share some interests and stories about themselves and then learn as much about the child as possible. In my course, I stress the importance of knowing the interests of your children in elementary and middle school in order to guide instruction. As I have stated before, my students are not ethnographers but they do use an ethnographic perspective when interviewing children.

Interviews with children are usually broken into different parts. First, try to develop rapport and make the child comfortable. Second, share information about yourself through storytelling in order to get the child to do the same. In my experience with my students, the final part of the conversation was a discussion of the essays that the child would write and how to make a list of the topics (Figure 4.4).

Beginning the Interview

The beginning of the interview is the most important part. Some of my students would begin interviewing in the native language of the child. Others would connect with the activities that interested the child, such as video games. Understanding the situation of being an English learner was another way to break the ice. Handing over the interview to the child and explicitly telling them that they would be the teacher was a good strategy. In the next example my student attended the same school as the child:

> Coincidentally, the school I went to observe is the elementary
> school I attended as a child and I felt that it was a good way to
> begin the conversation with Lindsay. As soon as I mentioned this
> fact to Lindsay her expression immediately changed. Her eyes were
> sparkling, eager to ask questions of when I went to school there and
> if some of my teachers were still around. I told her that only one of
> my teachers is still here and that was my kindergarten teacher. She

FIGURE 4.4. Example of a Topic List, Written with Invented Spelling by a 4th-Grade Boy

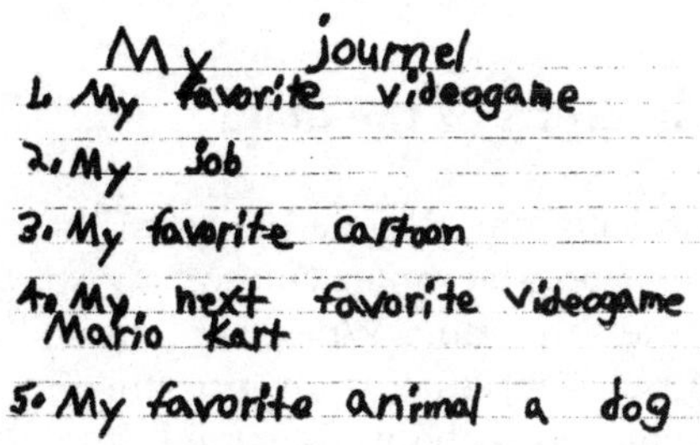

My journel
1. My favorite videogame
2. My Job
3. My favorite Cartoon
4. My, next favorite videogame Mario Kart
5. My favortie animal a dog

said she had started kinder here too and that her teacher was still here too. (Katey)

Another good strategy to use with children is to emphasize that the child is to be the teacher during the interview. For example, my students asked children to help them with their homework assignment for the university. This worked well for two of my students:

I conducted an interview with Jorge in the office of his grandmother's house. I asked him if he would help me with my homework. "What? Me, help you with your homework!" Jorge was shocked. I then explained to him that it is an assignment that my professor/teacher gave to me and that doing this assignment would help me in becoming a teacher. He said, "Oh, okay." (Luz)

Her face reveals that she is excited when I tell her she will tell me about herself and that she will be the teacher who is teaching me what I do not know. I tell her she will create a list, and on another day she will choose a topic from the list and will write a story about it. (Audrey)

Many of my students connected with the child by sharing similar experiences. In the next example, my student discovered that the child's parents were from El Salvador:

During that conversation I found out that both of our parents were from El Salvador. I talked to him about the time I visited El Salvador and the food I like to eat there. It was so exciting to find out that we had something in common. I think that by having a natural conversation with Sergio I was able to help him get comfortable enough to open up to me and talk about anything. Through this process I learned a lot about Sergio's interests and how to get him excited about writing by talking to him about his favorite things to do. (Sandy)

Discovering the Interests of the Child

If my student quickly found something that interested the child, the interview began on a positive note. One of my students interviewed a 9-year-old boy in the 4th grade. When she entered the home, he was playing a video game. Using that as an introduction, my student began the interview with questions about his game:

Javier was sitting in front of the television in the living room playing a video game. I greeted him as I entered and he said hello without taking his eyes off the TV set. His mother then asked Javier to turn the game off and signaled him to go to the kitchen where I was setting up. I took advantage of him playing his video game to get our conversation going. I asked him what game he was playing in which he responded, "Call of Duty 4." I proceeded to ask him about the game, such as what was the object of the game, why he liked to play it, if he played the game often and if there were any other games he liked to play. It was a real ice-breaker because he instantly opened up to me and was enthused to talk about everything and anything about his enjoyment of playing video games. (Nelly)

Another student did an interview with a 2nd-grade boy who also loved video games:

My case study student was able to write excellent journal entries because he was permitted to write about topics that interested him. Antonio loves video games. He plays them a lot when he's at home and with his cousins. He looks up to one of his cousins who he believes is a master video game player. He says that he teaches him new moves. Antonio also does gardening on the weekends for his grandma and gets paid $8.00. He saves his money to buy video games. He says that he likes his older brother sometimes because they also have fun playing video games. His favorite place is [Chuck E. Cheese] because he can play arcades and eat pizza. I then told him that I want him to write his own journal entries, and that he could choose whatever topic he liked. He asked me if he could write about video games. (Ysela)

FIGURE 4.5. Essay Example: "My Next Favorite Videogame Mario Kart"

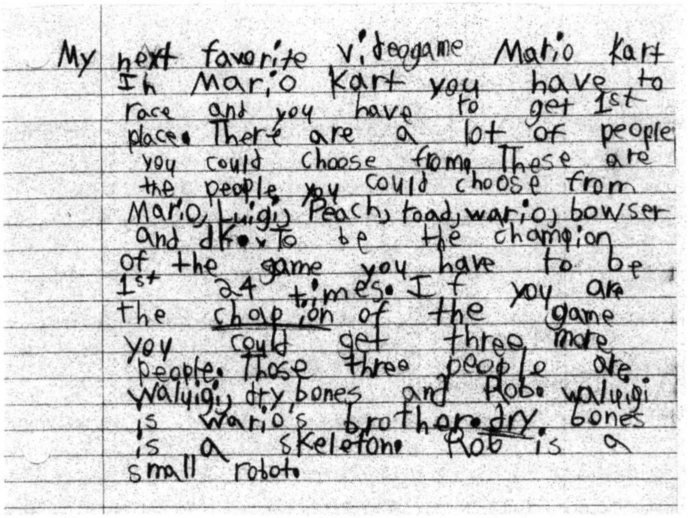
My next favorite videogame Mario Kart
In Mario Kart you have to
race and you have to get 1st
place. There are a lot of people
you could choose from. These are
the people you could choose from
Mario, Luigi, Peach, toad, wario, bowser
and dk. To be the champion
of the game you have to be
1st 24 times. If you are
the chap ion of the game
you could get three more
people. Those three people are
Waluigi, dry bones and Rob. waluigi
is wario's brother. dry bones
is a skeleton. Rob is a
small robot.

Antonio wrote five essays with two of them about video games: "My Favorite Videogame" and "My Next Favorite Videogame Mario Kart." In writing about Mario Kart, Antonio illustrated his in-depth knowledge of this game and how to play it. He knew the characters' names (Mario, Luigi, Peach, and Toad, to mention only a few) and how you become the "champion" of the game. (Figure 4.5)

Donald Graves (1983) explained how important it is for educators to "know the child." He challenged teachers in his seminars to list the names of their children and their interests. The task for teachers was to make a list of the students in their classrooms and then include experiences and interests. Teachers at elementary and middle schools with relatively small class sizes and a significant and ongoing amount of time with their students can do it if they realize how important it is to know the "unique territories of information about the children" (1983, p. 23).

CHILDREN IN ESL CLASSES/ENGLISH LEARNERS AS CHILD INFORMANTS

Another complication with interviewing arises with children whose native language is not English. My student who was able to speak Mandarin conducted the following interview at the child's home. I'm not sure if the student would have shared this much if my student had not spoken the same language. My student wrote in her report that when she interviewed the teacher at school, who did not speak Mandarin, she was told that the child was quiet and shy in class. However, my student found that she was talkative and outgoing:

> Meilin excitedly told me, "Every summer I go back to Shanghai and it's my favorite. I get to see my grandma, aunt, uncle, and a lot of cousins. I play with them but they don't play with me because they are older. I have a cousin in China and she has a son. He is a small baby that is 3 years old. He likes to bite but he don't bite anybody but people." I asked her what else she did in the summer and she said they sometimes go to the beach. She then resumed talking about China and said, "We go for 7 days. I go back to China and I buy something for my grandma like seaweed, tea, and little presents." (Catherine)

It is more difficult when you do not share the language of the child you are interviewing. For example, Vanessa, an English-only student, had difficulty engaging a child, whose native language was Vietnamese, during the interview. Vanessa used the suggestion I gave my students, which was to share her own stories first, but somehow the interview did not go well. The interview was conducted at the child's school:

> I gave her a piece of paper and asked her to write as many story ideas as possible. I was surprised that she struggled for ideas because she was so talkative with friends. I reminded her of the topics I had shared with her and she began to tell me that she went to the mall over the weekend. She then asked me if she could write about going to the mall. I told her yes, and that she could write about anything she wanted to share. She wrote down a few ideas, one including going to the mall and another of her own trip to Canada. I asked her if she needed more time to think or if she needed some assistance. She told me immediately that she was out of ideas. I began to ask her questions about what she does over summer or winter break, what she does after school, what other vacations she had been on and if she had any interesting family stories. She finished her topic list, even though she struggled with ideas. I felt that at any moment she was going to ask me if her ideas were "right." I am not sure if she understood that I wanted her to write about anything she wanted. (Vanessa)

Since most of my students were bilingual, many had school experiences with bilingual education that were similar to those of the child they interviewed.

Interviewing child informants is complex. When conducting ethnographic interviews with children, all the cautions that have been mentioned (Figure 4.2) must be taken into consideration. When we interview child informants who are not native English speakers, another complication arises. Ethnographers who explore cultures in foreign lands must first learn the language. It made sense then to expect that students who know the language of the child will elicit a more descriptive interview than someone who does not. In this next example, Kyoung, who spoke Korean, explains this in her report. She chose a Korean child in 5th grade for this assignment. The interview took place in the classroom after school:

> We spoke in Korean, which is the native language for both of us. That appeared to help Hana become more relaxed, since we could talk to each other in a more comfortable way. Talking in English is something we both could do but it takes more concentration for us. I asked Hana in what language she preferred to speak and she told me, "Korean is easier." Since we shared the same cultural background, that also seemed to help build rapport between us. I told Hana there was no right or wrong answer to my questions. My questions, I said, would help me to get to know her better. I started the interview by asking Hana to tell me about a typical school day, starting with when she wakes up. (Kyoung)

Kyoung began the interview with an ethnographic question about a "typical" day. Her report illustrated that she understood the answer from the perspective of a child of Korean parents and understood the discipline, the commitment to homework, and the desire to please her parents:

> I encouraged Hana to tell me about a typical day at school. "I never forget my homework," she told me in a proud voice. She likes to read about math and science and likes it when those subjects are the first subjects of the day. Hana told me that in the afternoon, she often had to study language arts but she did not enjoy that subject. "I don't see the point in reading or writing about fiction," she said. "I like to focus on what is real." Hana said she likes to get to the point and not talk and talk about unimportant things. I learned a lot from this interview with Hana. She is a very well-disciplined child in her studies, and I am sure she gets this sense of discipline

from her parents. "Do the right thing" is a saying Hana has learned very well. Hana wants to make her parents proud of her. Like many girls in Korean families, Hana does not want to make any mistakes. (Kyoung)

INTERVIEWING CHILDREN AT HOME

Just as the child interview is incomplete without an observation at the school, it is also incomplete without a home visit. When Kyoung visited Hana's home, she brought fried chicken and interviewed the grandfather, also in Korean. They discussed Korean politics and when asked about Hana's strengths and weaknesses, the grandfather praised her work in school but said she was stubborn and not willing to change her mind. He said he was glad his granddaughter was born in Korea because Korean children born in the United States become too American too quickly. Kyoung was given a tour of the home and noticed that in Hana's bedroom there were few fictional books but many on math and science in both English and Korean. In her report, Kyoung concluded:

The most surprising thing about my home visit was how Hana's personality had changed. In school, she is formal and usually unemotional. At home, she is much more relaxed and friendly, much more of an extrovert. Perhaps she feels happier talking in Korean to someone, like me, who shares her culture. When I asked Hana to describe her typical school day, I observed that her day was mostly about her duties in school. She had to bring her homework to school. She had to study hard. She had to be diligent. She did not seem to have a lot of fun in school. In that sense, perhaps Hana is a typical Korean American student. She is driven. She wants to succeed. She does not want to embarrass her family. She does not choose to speak in English, because she speaks Korean better. If she speaks English, she is more likely to make a mistake. And Hana does not like making mistakes. (Kyoung)

The interview by Kyoung illustrates that interviews conducted at home and at school can show very different aspects of the child. Both are important. Additionally, Kyoung illustrates that interviews conducted in the same language as the informant may be more revealing and add more information. It also could be that interviewers who speak the same language engender trust faster.

CHILDREN WITH SPECIAL NEEDS

The ethnographic interviews that my students conducted were usually not with children with special needs. The few times that a child with special needs was interviewed was when a student was in the Division of Special Education or when the student teacher chose a child that they knew well. That was the case when Adriana chose Michael, whom she had known for many years.

In Adriana's case, she knew the child well because he was her neighbor. Over the years she had watched him grow and they developed a good relationship. When she went to his school to observe him, she found that he participated in all the events but remained quiet during discussions, even in small groups. She also noticed that he was very sociable and got along well with his peers. When he came over to her house to work on his essays, he would be talkative with Adriana and her husband. She wrote, "I found working with him an easy task since he was always full of energy and enthusiasm." She did notice that he had trouble sitting still for long. He even wrote his essays standing up. The mother said that the school suspected that her child had ADD or ADHD in 3rd grade but when the school psychologist tested him, it was found that he did not have either. His mother said that he was just a very active boy. At first, Adriana was surprised that he had no problems writing his essays. She wrote:

> I guess in my mind I had a preconceived notion that if a child received intervention he or she would be slower with their writing or not like to write at all. This child said that writing was easy and added that since he had to write about things he knew about he could write fast. (Adriana)

This points to another advantage of engaging children in ethnographic interviews. When we use interviews, our "preconceived notions" are challenged and we learn how to see from a different perspective; we become more aware with respect to the child, the child's home, and the parents. In this case, the child, who did not have severe special needs but did receive intervention in reading, writing, and math, was able to write when given a choice of topics and given a chance to choose the area where he would write. Although scoring below grade level on his spelling, the rough drafts that he wrote were filled with stories about a trip to SeaWorld, going to see *Ice Age 2* at the movies, attending a Lakers basketball game at Staples Center, bowling with his mom, his 10th-birthday party, and the best hiding place while playing hide-and-go-seek.

SUMMARY

Some ethnographic techniques when interviewing children are to let the child be the teacher, play dumb, repeat information for more clarification, and listen instead of talk. Although difficult, giving up control, letting the child lead the interview, and making the interview more open and fluid are suggestions for teachers interviewing children. When teachers understand that knowing the interests of the child are critical to guide instruction, then ethnographic techniques for interviewing children become important.

Activities to Explore the Ideas

1. Interview a child. Do you find that it is difficult not to guide the interview in a specific direction? Are all the questions about what *you* want to know, or can you ask open-ended questions that help you understand how the child views their everyday life? How might you conduct the interview so that you can enter the child's world?
2. How might you discover the interests of a child? Begin an interview with a child by telling them stories of your life and your interests. Does it help the child to share when you share your stories first?

Suggested Readings

Corsaro, W. (1981). Entering the child's world: Research strategies for field entry and data collection in a preschool setting. In J. Green & C. Wallat (Eds.), *Ethnography and language in educational settings* (pp. 117–146). Norwood, NJ: Ablex.

> Bill Corsaro entered a preschool as one of the kids in order to study children's language and activity. This is a perceptive look into the world of children as it details how to do ethnography in unusual settings.

Tammivaara, J., & Enright, D. S. (1986). On eliciting information: Dialogues with child informants. *Anthropology & Education Quarterly, 17,* 218–238.

> This insightful article on interviews with schoolchildren is written from an ethnographic perspective and considers the difference between interviewing children and adults.

CHAPTER 5

Interviewing Teachers
in Teacher Education

It is weird how learning to "teacher talk" is for me like learning a new language. (Sue, a student teacher during her kindergarten placement, as cited in Frank, 1999, p. 27)

Ethnographic interviews enable novice teachers to explore the actions and talk of experienced teachers in more depth. When student teachers are learning from cooperating or mentor teachers, they are sometimes afraid of looking inept or unknowledgeable. However, when they can see themselves as "ethnographers" going into a foreign land to learn a new language, they become more comfortable with the procedure. They become scientists and anthropologists and lose the sense of being ashamed of not knowing and, instead, take on the role of investigators.

Additionally, the frequent observations that student teachers engage in before beginning to teach make more sense when they discuss what they have observed with the cooperating teacher. They begin to understand the objectives and the long-range goals that teachers have in mind. Student teachers need some way of understanding the thinking of their cooperating teacher in order to learn how to make decisions like a teacher. This communication depends on the relationship, or rapport, that is built between the two. As student teachers engage in ethnographic interviews with cooperating teachers, they begin to understand this "member knowledge." Using these ethnographic practices that see classrooms as cultures, beginning teachers might better transition from thinking like students to thinking like teachers.

There are two types of students described in this chapter. The first type refers to the students I supervised in the UCSB Teacher Education Program while they were student teaching (identified here as student teachers). These were the nine student teachers I describe in *Ethnographic Eyes* (Frank, 1999), the main focus of which was classroom observations. The second type includes students who attended Cal State LA's Charter

College of Education and who were taking my course in writing instruction before they carried out their student teaching (identified here as preservice teachers).

Both groups observed classrooms, and when they did, they usually observed smoothly running classrooms, managed by experienced teachers. Although it was beneficial to observe these kinds of classrooms, it was often difficult to understand everything the teacher did to get the classroom running so efficiently. As the beginning teachers observed in classrooms, they realized quickly that they did not have the same expertise as their cooperating or master teachers.

Beginning teachers sometimes try to make up for their lack of expertise by copying the actions and talk of the teachers they watch. By doing that, they begin to take on the activity of teaching, but without examining why they do what they do. They still do not understand the teacher thinking that provides the basis for the teacher's practice. By conducting ethnographic interviews, new teachers can think of their cooperating teacher as an "informant" who can give access to this new culture of teaching for them. By interviewing through ethnography, their classroom observations make more sense. In addition, they don't have to think of themselves as students but as scientists, anthropologists, and ethnographers discovering and describing new cultures.

As in other professions such as medicine or law, beginning practitioners in teaching do not understand or communicate in the vernacular of their field. When my student teachers and preservice teachers interviewed cooperating teachers from their perspectives as students, they did not know what questions to ask. If one of my students entered a classroom and began asking many questions, they felt that it reinforced their inexpertness, their sense of not belonging in the classroom. They felt as if it labeled them as being unintelligent or uninformed. In order to offset this problem, I explained to them that the role of the ethnographer is not that of a student but, rather, that of an anthropologist trying to gather information about a different way of living. I thought this would be a perfect role for novice teachers who were not familiar with the culture of teaching.

HOW ETHNOGRAPHIC INTERVIEWS EXPLAIN OBSERVATIONS

One of my student teachers at UCSB, Aurora, used an ethnographic interview with her cooperating teacher. Through this interview, she began to understand the thinking behind some of the decisions of her cooperating teacher. At the beginning of the school year, one of the questions she asked was, "What are the main considerations you thought of when setting up the room this way?" The answer to this question brought out a wealth of information that student teachers might not have considered. The cooperating teacher talked of the physical constraints of electrical sockets for computers and the placement of the screen for the overhead projector determining where the "front" of the room was going to be. Aurora wrote:

> She has the desks set up in groups (mostly groups of 5) because she likes the students to work in cooperative groups. She placed her desk in the far corner because she seldom uses it. (I've only seen her sit at it a couple of times, and that has always been after school.) Even during reading or writing time, she chooses to sit at an empty student desk so as not to be away from the students. The desk works well in this area because there is a supply closet next to it. She has a couch set up right when you walk in the room, and she has set it up around bookcases to serve as a class library and reading center. (Aurora, as quoted in Frank, 1999)

Drawing from this interview, Aurora was able to ask her cooperating teacher more questions about cooperative learning and grouping her students. She learned how this particular teacher was thinking about arranging the furniture in the classroom (mostly groups of 5) according to her beliefs of how students learn best (using cooperative learning much of the time). She also learned how important reading was to this teacher (placing a couch near the bookcases).

As the interview continued, Aurora was able to integrate her observations of the classroom with her interview. She became curious about why the walls were bare and discovered during the interview why this teacher did not decorate the room. She also realized that first impressions might not always be correct:

> On my first visit, the teacher had all of the bulletin boards (six in all) covered with colored paper and colorful borders, but nothing else on them. My first impression was that the room lacked a "theme" and needed more "stuff" on the walls and bulletin boards. I quickly came to understand there was a theme and that theme was "Student Work." The walls of this classroom are evolving daily and are being adorned with the work the students have done since the first day of school. This class is definitely a "student centered" classroom. This teacher did not feel it necessary to cover the walls and bulletin boards with her creations. She preferred to adorn them with the

work of her students. This is not an assumption, because I asked her about it. When the boards were still empty, I asked her what she planned on putting on them and she already knew exactly what would be going on each one, once the students completed those particular assignments. I was amazed at the thought and planning that went into each bulletin board. This was a great lesson for me because prior to witnessing this, I would have felt that every space should be filled on the first day of school with stuff! (Aurora, as quoted in Frank, 1999, p. 36)

Aurora also asked her cooperating teacher what she thought of team teaching, who the key people were that she should know in the school, what kinds of decisions she had to make about the curriculum prior to the start of school, what main events would be happening in 6th grade or in a reading group, and what she considered when forming a group. With all this information, the student teacher was able to understand the classroom from the teacher's perspective and see how this teacher was thinking about the students and making decisions about the curriculum. Although this student teacher might ultimately make different choices with her own classroom, she at least had a beginning understanding of many of the kinds of decisions that teachers need to make.

QUESTIONS FOR STUDENT TEACHERS TO ASK

It is helpful for student teachers interviewing cooperating teachers to ask grand tour questions (Spradley, 1979) during an ethnographic interview. For example, a classroom teacher might give the student teacher a grand tour of the room where they will both teach. Figure 5.1 presents a variety of questions to use to begin this grand tour. Learning about space, time, and events in the classroom will give the student teacher more information about how teachers practice their craft.

These guidelines for grand tour questions are helpful because in the beginning, when they are moving from being students to being teachers, student teachers often don't even know what questions to ask. They are unfamiliar with the language of teaching and rarely know how to talk like teachers. These questions guide them to discover ways to communicate with other teachers and learn their craft.

Not only do new teachers need to know how teachers talk, they will need to know how teachers think and make decisions. By taking a tour of the classroom and asking questions about people, activities, and objects,

FIGURE 5.1. Questions for Student Teachers to Ask

1. *Space*. Could you describe your classroom to me? How do you use the different bulletin boards on your walls?
2. *Time*. Could you describe the main things that happen during the school year?
3. *Events*. Can you tell me all the things that happen in a writing or reading conference? What happens during your reading instruction?
4. *People*. Can you tell me a little bit about the children in the classroom? What are some of the tasks that you assign to your parent helpers or your instructional aides?
5. *Activities*. How do activities vary at different times in the room? Do your children have free time to read and, if so, where do they do this?
6. *Objects*. Could you describe the tools children use during writing workshop? What are the mathematic manipulatives used for?

Source: Developed from Spradley, 1979

FIGURE 5.2. Types of Grand Tour Questions for Preservice Teachers

1. *Guided Grand Tour Question*. Could you show me around the classroom and tell me what kinds of decisions you made about each area? Could you tell me how you write up a lesson plan?
2. *Typical Grand Tour Question*. Could you describe a typical day in your classroom? Could you describe a typical period when the children are engaged in writing workshop?
3. *Specific Grand Tour Question*. Could you describe what will happen during a parent conference? Could you tell me all the things that happen on the first day of school?
4. *Task-Related Grand Tour Question*. Could you show me the stages that the children go through when they write an essay? Could you draw a map of your seating chart and tell me what decisions you made?

student teachers will begin to understand how teachers make decisions and how teachers prepare for the beginning of the year.

Elementary and middle school teachers often have long-range goals in mind when they begin to set up their classrooms in September. Guests who enter classrooms never see the preplanning that goes into teaching. Ethnographic interviews help new teachers understand this preparation. Spradley (1979) breaks apart the grand tour questions further into four categories (Figure 5.2), which may be useful for student teachers: typical, specific, guided, and task-related. These ideas may allow student teachers to generate their own questions.

My students at Cal State LA had not yet started student teaching so I considered them "preservice teachers." In my course they were expected to observe for 14 hours in an experienced teacher's classroom. I usually scheduled these observations with an exemplary teacher who I knew was practicing the same approach to writing I teach in my classroom, namely "writing workshop," an instructional approach advocated by Nancie Atwell (1987). When I asked my students to interview the teacher after the observation, they used the questions that were similar to the ones in Figures 5.1 and 5.2. (Can you describe a typical day in your classroom? What will happen on the first day of school until they leave on the last day? Can you give me an example of a peer conference? What goes on during a writing conference?)

My students loved interviewing these experienced teachers and soon created their own questions: How did you become interested in writing workshop? What is your rationale when you explain the writing workshop to your students' parents? For the most part, do the parents agree or disagree with the process? Would you recommend writing workshop to other districts? Why or why not? With all this freedom, how do you prepare for standardized tests?

QUESTIONS FOR PRESERVICE TEACHERS TO ASK

When I came to Cal State LA from Santa Barbara, I continued to teach students how to observe and interview from an ethnographic perspective. However, Cal State LA preservice teachers had less time with their cooperating teachers, observing in classrooms for only 14 hours. The observation assignment was focused on writing instruction. They did an ethnographic observation and then sat down with the teacher for an interview. The interviews were a combination of formal and informal conversations with teachers after the fieldnotes were collected.

My students asked me what questions to ask during the interviews, and although I gave them some ideas, I cautioned them that their questions would evolve from the observation and would be different depending on the classroom and their own individual interests. The questions that developed ranged from "Could you describe a typical day in your class?" and "What are all the ways space is used by the students in the classroom?" to questions more focused on writing workshop such as "How did you find out about writing workshop?" and "Where do you get your ideas for writing workshop?" If a student used the observation to guide the interview, the questions were more specific: "What are the spoons for on the homework chart? What are the orange tickets for? How many journals do they have?"

Some of the interview questions were peculiar to writing instruction. For example, when one of my students asked, "Is there an area you perceive as needing improvement in the writer's workshop with your students?" the teacher answered,

> Yes. Peer conferencing is an art, but my students don't see that. They don't know enough to ask a good question. They're not critical enough. They don't take the peer conferences seriously. Sometimes they just socialize or fool around. (Margaret)

In this way, preservice teachers collected data from practitioners concerning theoretical concepts about peer conferencing during writing workshop that I taught them in my class. They were hearing "practice wisdom," or knowledge gained from experience, from classroom teachers, for example, about how peer conferences may be beneficial but were also difficult to implement in real classrooms.

ETHNOGRAPHY BASED ON EVIDENCE

As I discussed in Chapter 1, when carrying out ethnography-based investigations, both observations and interviews are necessary. One complements the other. When I was at UCSB, I gave my students suggestions to follow when they were observing classrooms. I wanted the student teachers to know that they would be entering as strangers into a community that had been built up over a long period of time. They would be entering an ongoing stream of activity, crossing the river in the middle. They could look down from a bridge and watch the water rushing by beneath them but in no way would they be able to really understand what was happening unless they jumped in and swam down the river with the kids in the classroom. Even then, they would be missing events at the source.

When teaching preservice teachers at Cal State LA, I still encouraged my students to observe from an ethnographic perspective and use the observation as a springboard for the ethnographic interview. My colleague Fred Uy and I did a study with preservice teachers to examine how they used ethnographic fieldnotes when observing classrooms. We found that most preservice teachers during the data collection period were able to write descriptive fieldnotes about what was happening during writing instruction without making interpretations or evaluations based on their own personal perspectives (Frank & Uy, 2004).

In the following example, we compared fieldnotes from two of our preservice teachers, Barry and Valerie, to illustrate the difference between ethnographic observation and regular observation. They observed the same classroom during the same event, but Barry had not had any instruction on ethnographic observations. Valerie had already taken my class in which she engaged in the lessons on ethnographic observations. Barry did not record the talk of the teacher or children and, because he was not recording conversations verbatim, his fieldnotes illustrate how he failed to learn as much as possible by not collecting enough evidence. He filtered what was heard through his own interpretation and then summarized it.

Valerie observed the classroom on the same day as Barry but was using an ethnographic approach to observation. It can be seen, comparing these two sets of fieldnotes side by side, that while Barry's notes were compressed and *described* the talk, Valerie recorded as many as possible of the actual words that the teacher and children used—she was collecting more information from the classroom to use as evidence for her interpretation. For example, Barry's fieldnotes during one moment in this classroom (9:50 a.m.) contain one line, while Valerie's contain 14 lines:

Barry's Fieldnotes for 9:50 a.m. 10/17 (Author's Chair):

9:50 During Author's chair, I notice the papers have become more descriptive.

Valerie's Fieldnotes for 9:50 a.m. 10/17 (Author's Chair):

9:50 Teacher rings bell. "Okay it is authors chair time"
      Students get up push in chairs and take their compositions along with them to the rug area. Teacher pulls out a log and calls out a name of student and title of story. "Your [*sic*] Done!" a student remarked.

S—Comments:
      "I like when you said . . ."
      "I like your brother's curly hair."

S—Questions:
      "How old are your brothers?
      "What are the names of your parents and brothers?

Teacher: "What is a name going to do for you? Names are important to inform us. Character 'Viola Swamp' ugly name. Think of a swamp is ugly and dirty. Well the character plays a . . . that is mean and ugly. So that's why names are important"

Comparing these two sets of fieldnotes illustrates that writing as much of the classroom talk as possible allows preservice teachers opportunities to see from the teacher's perspective later, during the interpretation stage. Observers who use ethnographic techniques see "informants" who are engaged in "cultural rituals," and in doing so are able to see what is actually happening and not what is assumed to be happening. The difference between writing about the talk and writing the talk verbatim means the difference between glancing quickly at a classroom from an outside perspective and seeing or understanding it from the emic, or insider's, perspective.

By interpreting at the same time, Barry was trying to describe the classroom in his fieldnotes ("I notice the papers have become more descriptive"), Barry missed an opportunity to observe how a teacher teaches descriptive writing. In this instance, the teacher gives her students a useful writing strategy, telling her students that writers can name characters so that readers will understand their personalities. She draws on Viola Swamp, an ugly and mean substitute teacher from *Miss Nelson is Missing* (Allard & Marshall, 1977), as an example.

During 4 days of observations, Barry only took six pages of fieldnotes and then wrote his interpretation of writing workshop in his summary:

The loose atmosphere brought a high noise level. I am not sure students were able to write effectively with the loud noise. Student collaboration changed into visiting and drawing pictures instead of proofreading and revising papers. I wonder if the writer's workshop time could be better focused in a more directed manner. (Barry)

Valerie, on the other hand, took 42 pages of fieldnotes during her 4 days of observing, which were all focused on the conversations during writing instruction. Her conclusions about this same teacher's writing workshop were quite different:

Now I have a more accurate understanding of how to proceed with creating an atmosphere like Megan's in my own classroom some day. I feel confident enough that as soon as I get my own classroom I will start a writer's workshop as soon as I start teaching. I noticed that just reading the information in a book is not the same as witnessing an actual session. (Valerie)

Valerie was able to look at informants acting in various roles and relationships as she found that "everyone knew just what was expected of them, so they kept the noise level down." Additionally, Valerie noticed how this teacher used the language of writers: "I really like how Megan used technical terms when answering children." Valerie implied that there was a role reversal in writing workshop as she concluded her summary with

> What struck me the most from observing this class was that the workshop ran so smoothly and everyone was learning from it. It was almost as if it was being run by the students. (Valerie)

Not only did she observe what writing workshop looked like in a classroom but she was also able to visualize herself as a writing workshop teacher in the future. Her ethnographic fieldnotes gave her the opportunity to see this classroom from the perspective of the teacher in order to understand what was being accomplished and why.

Using an ethnographic approach for observations and interviews, preservice teachers collected evidence in the form of fieldnotes and then used this evidence to summarize their interpretations or to interview the teacher. These observers were using quotations from their fieldnotes as evidence for their interpretations of what happened during writing instruction or for the basis of their interviews. They were writing and speaking from an informed position as participant observers who had spent time with one teacher. For example, one student explained what she noticed about one teacher's writing conference and used quotations from her fieldnotes:

> She gave positive feedback that I think helped the students reflect on their own pieces. With Student #1, her remarks were both guiding and encouraging: "What is the main idea? Good sentence . . . Good detail . . . What did you think when that happened? How about a sentence or two where you explain it?" With Student #2, she asked a lot of questions that helped the writer develop her piece: "How are you going to give me examples of what that is like? How does your monster move? How are you going to scare me? Help me to imagine." She makes the writer aware of her audience. She gives suggestions about what to include. (Connie)

In Connie's summary, the description of the writing conference centered on how the teacher helped students expand their writing by giving attention to detail and to questions readers might ask. She drew on the evidence collected in the fieldnotes to give examples of how the teacher spoke during a conference. Connie also noticed that the conference context was a place where writers "reflect on their own pieces" and that the resource used to teach writing was the student's own piece.

It is interesting to note Connie's point of view in this summary. Instead of explaining from her own position as a preservice teacher and student, she has taken up the concerns of the teacher and focused on how the questions that the teacher used in the writing conference were based on the needs of the student. Connie draws from the observation an awareness of how teachers engage in instructional conversations depending on what the child needs at the moment.

HOW INTERVIEWS ANSWER QUESTIONS FROM OBSERVATIONS

Using an ethnographic approach allows preservice teachers opportunities to collaborate with more-experienced teachers during ethnographic interviews. Of the 42 preservice teachers in our study at Cal State LA, 40 engaged in interviews. Observers became skilled notetakers, but until they had a chance to interview the teacher, the fieldnotes presented some questions for them. As one preservice teacher wrote in her summary, "Interviewing and observation are both important. One is not complete without the other." For example, in one instance a preservice teacher observed a child covering her mouth during a period called author's chair and questioned the teacher about this child:

> There were several things that I needed [the teacher] to explain to me. One was, why did Juliana cover her mouth when she spoke in the author's chair? [In the interview, the teacher explained that] Juliana, a very shy child, had just started using English this past year. It was her first time in the author's chair. [The teacher] was thrilled that she had come so far. (Melody)

In another case, a preservice teacher recorded in his fieldnotes how the teacher pointed to the students instead of calling them by name: "When I point to you you'll come back to my desk and get this piece of paper. (She doesn't call on students—she's pointing to them.)" In his summary, he explained how the interview clarified this observation:

> Much of the time [the teacher] will point instead of calling out a student's name. When I asked her about this, she said, "It's to make

sure the students are paying attention to me with their eyes as well as their ears." (Nate)

In this way, preservice teachers used interviews to answer questions about what the teachers were doing during the observation as well as why they were doing certain things.

When preservice teachers talked to master teachers it gave the novices opportunities to discuss teaching and learning on an experiential level with practitioners. Additionally, my students asked questions about strategies that were used in a context that both had witnessed, instead of discussing abstract concepts at the university. When asked if the class had been a GATE (Gifted and Talented) class, the teacher was able to expand this observation and guide the preservice teacher to a more child-centered view of instruction as she explained how writing workshop is beneficial for urban classrooms with a range of resources. She answered:

> No, I do not have the GATE class. I have quite a range of abilities. You may notice that many of my students are English Language Learners. Writing workshop is good for them because it is a low anxiety, process approach to learning writing conventions and form. (Carol)

HOW ETHNOGRAPHIC QUESTIONS EXPAND TEACHER ANSWERS

Drawing on the ethnographic questions that were used for the observations at UCSB, when I came to Cal State LA, I devised similar questions for the interviews that my students would ask of the teachers that they observed (Figure 5.3). The teacher's answer to the question about two teachers talking uncovered more information about the writing workshop:

> Of course, it would depend on the opinions of both teachers. If both teachers were pro [Writing] Workshop, you'd hear them sing the praise of the program. They would insist that it's the best time of the day for them and their students because it's the time when students are actively engaged. Every teacher I've spoken to who loves [Writing] Workshop still has issues regarding management. The teachers all include the basic fundamentals, but they each have their own management style. That's where your individual teaching style comes in. If both teachers were negative toward [Writing] Workshop, they would complain that the program has no structure and that students should not be "in charge." Also, these teachers would say that there is no time during the day. They would argue

FIGURE 5.3. Ethnographic Questions After Observations

1. I noticed you began each writing workshop with a minilesson. How do you decide what to teach during these lessons?
2. I observed peer conferences in your classroom. How did you teach the children to participate in these conferences?
3. Can you explain the sharing process used as the students are seated on the rug?
4. My fieldnotes show that you conducted many writing conferences. What is your instructional goal when you are engaging the children in writing conferences?
5. If I listened to two teachers talking about writing workshop what would I hear them say?

that the workshop doesn't address state standards or the state STAR test [Standardized Testing and Reporting]. They would complain that conventions and skills are not being taught. (Carol)

Understanding the philosophical argument going on in the field concerning various approaches to education, such as using writing workshop for writing instruction, helps students see that there is never "one right way" in teaching and that there are multiple opinions concerning instruction. Preservice teachers could now predict that if they used writing workshop with their own students, they would have to be prepared to defend this instructional strategy. However, this question also offered the teacher a chance to explain further her feelings about writing workshop. In doing so, the interviewer had succeeded in getting the informant to expand on the subject and talk more about the topic. The teacher continued with her answer:

If you have two teachers—one in favor of [Writing] Workshop and one interested in implementing the program, there would be a lot of questions. The one interested would wonder how to get started. How do you fit it into an already busy day? How do you conference with all the students? How do you keep "control" of behavior? The teacher responding would probably admit that those are good questions. When I respond to others who question me, I always tell them that it won't be perfect the first time. I'm constantly adjusting and modifying according to the group I have that year. I learn something new every year. I would tell them they will probably go outside their comfort zone because teachers love control, but it works. I would respond that students aren't "in control." They have choice, but the teacher still directs the work and learning. As far as the limited time, I agree that there isn't enough time, but I would argue that it's the most productive time of our day. There's a big group of teachers who like [Writing] Workshop, but feel overwhelmed. I always tell those teachers, look at the main parts of [Writing] Workshop. Figure out a management plan, and get started. (Carol)

SUMMARY

Ethnographic interviews can be great vehicles for informing beginning teachers about why inservice teachers do what they do. By looking over fieldnotes and hearing interpretations of what was happening from another perspective, experienced and novice teachers can together reflect on what happened, how it happened, and whether or not it was successful. Interviews expand upon observations for preservice teachers and also validate for the experienced teachers that what they are doing is significant and valued. Instead of looking from textbook practices and personal experience alone, ethnographic observers can draw from their own research data to ask experts about practices they have seen working successfully in classrooms.

Activities to Explore the Ideas

1. Observe an elementary or middle school classroom for a week, being sure to observe at the same time each day. Take fieldnotes of as much of the talk as possible. Reread the fieldnotes and write a summary of what you think was happening.
2. Then ask the teacher if you can interview him/her about your observation. Use your fieldnotes to prepare questions, remembering the ideas presented in this book. Then write another summary and compare it with the first.
3. Interview a principal or vice-principal of a school. Ask if you can tape the interview. Then listen to the recording and see if there is a difference between how the principal talked and how the teacher talked.

Suggested Readings

There have been many studies done that focus on classroom talk. Listed here are works by three of the most influential authors on the topic.

Cazden, C. B. (2001). *Classroom discourse: The language of teaching and learning.* Portsmouth, NH: Heinemann.

Edwards, A. D., & Westgate, D. P. G. (1994). *Investigating classroom talk* (2nd ed.). London: Falmer.

Erickson, F. (1982). Classroom discourse as improvisation: Relationships between academic task structure and social participation in lessons. In L. C. Wilkinson (Ed.), *Communicating in the classroom* (pp. 153–182). New York: Academic Press.

CHAPTER 6

Ethnography in the Classroom

I think how we learn in our class is to think about how we do our
questions instead of just going the easy way and writing down the
answer. What I mean by this is, say we had a fraction, we wouldn't just
multiply the two and say we're finished. We would say how we thought
about it and how we came up with that answer. Basically we go
through the process. (Brad, a 5th grader, as quoted in Yeager, Floriani,
& Green, 1998, p. 123)

How does ethnography help students in classrooms? By learning how to
do ethnographic interviews, classroom students learn that printed texts
are not the only source of information and that people in the community
can also be a resource for learning about the world. Teachers using
ethnography in the classroom encourage their students to use another
person as a resource and to conduct interviews to obtain primary sources
of information. Teachers using ethnography in the classroom ask students
to use the interview process as one of the many ways to collect information
when writing reports. Students interview members of the community or
experts in the field they are researching. One teacher had her students
interview football coaches, mayors, and zoo managers. The students
learn how to develop a list of questions, tape-record the interview, and
transcribe the audiotape to investigate what was discovered.

When students learn the fundamentals of ethnography, they learn
to approach all experiences in particular ways. For example, when approaching a piece of text, perhaps a social studies text, they might ask
themselves, "Who wrote this? From what perspective is the author speaking? What language is in use (historical, mathematical, scientific)? What
are key words and phrases?"

Asking students to become ethnographers of their own classrooms is
not a new concept. Shirley Brice Heath (1983) was one of the first educators to explore the benefits of using ethnography with teachers and students as a tool for learning. Egan-Robertson and Bloome (1998) extended

this theory as they showed how students become researchers of their own communities through ethnography.

In Santa Barbara, Beth Yeager (1999) used ethnographic inquiry with her 5th-grade students as they learned to become historians, mathematicians, scientists, and artists. Using an ethnographic perspective with students enabled them to "be able to inquire into their thinking, to examine their procedures and processes for learning, and to be able to understand the ways in which the class community was being constructed through the ways they interacted with others" (Yeager, Floriani, & Green, 1998, p. 116). In describing how ethnography is used in classrooms, Dixon, Frank, and Green (1999) state that ethnography can be used as a tool for learning:

> Some teachers have explicitly used both the theory (theories of culture) and the practices (observing, recording, and interpreting patterns of life) of ethnography. These teachers help students learn how to observe from a point of view, to take notes, to interpret data, to talk from evidence grounded in their everyday actions and those of others, and to take up the language of ethnography. By using ethnography as an instructional resource, these teachers have helped students to engage in inquiry across academic content areas as well as to reflect on what and how they are learning in their classrooms. (p. 6)

STUDENTS AS ETHNOGRAPHERS

Teachers who want to use ethnography in their classrooms can help students learn the difference between description and interpretation when taking fieldnotes. When introducing ethnography, teachers might display a photograph of a classroom, show a video of a classroom activity, or ask students to observe other students playing a game. Then students can discuss ways of dividing "note-taking" (description) from "note-making" (interpretation). For example, Figure 6.1 is a photograph of a student in 7th grade. If it was projected on the screen for students to observe, their descriptions and interpretations might look like this:

Note-taking
Male child wearing glasses sitting at desk.
LA written on his brown cap.
Child is writing in a notebook.
He is right handed and using a pencil.
His head is leaning on his left hand.

FIGURE 6.1. Child in 7th Grade. When introducing ethnography, teachers might display a photograph and then students can discuss ways of dividing "note-taking" (description) from "note-making" (interpretation).

Note-making
What is he writing?
Does LA signify Los Angeles or Louisiana?
Is this a classroom?
Why is he sitting in the corner?
Is he happy or sad?

Many of the interpretive note-making comments are questions. The goal when using ethnography for observing or interviewing is to generate more questions in order to describe what is happening with more detail and depth.

The ability to reflect back on the fieldnotes and gain greater insights into what was happening is a process that would benefit students, not only for research purposes, but also for other learning experiences. In fact, all techniques used in ethnography (collecting data, interviewing, observing, analyzing, categorizing, organizing, comparing, contrasting, and writing up) can be used as tools for learning other subjects.

Teachers might have students do a comparison from microanalysis (looking at what was said and done) to macroanalysis (considering the whole context). Videos that use successive orders of magnitude, from the Milky Way to cell walls of a leaf (e.g., The Power of Ten Web site), help illustrate how more information is gained as the point of view of the observer changes. This idea is a key way of thinking in social studies, which challenges students to see themselves as part of a larger whole and to imagine how it is for members of other societies to see themselves.

Furthermore, students might analyze the fieldnotes by searching for repeated patterns (e.g., homework) or themes (e.g., how time manages the structure of the school day). Students could reflect on these patterns and themes in order to understand or initiate change. Transcripts could be created from fieldnotes so that students could see how "talk" is a major mode of learning. Other artifacts that students and teachers use during the day could be examined in this same way in order to look critically at what is being used in school and how.

Having students become ethnographers of their own classrooms allows students to examine why things are happening in school. They take ownership of the events in their lives, standing back and reflecting on what they do at school, who they do it with, what is said, what actions they take, and why they act as they do. In this way, the events of their academic lives take on more meaning. They develop a kind of "wide-awakeness" (Calkins, 1986) as they notice and reflect back on their experiences and record their community life. Involving these students as co-researchers in this inquiry means that students assume the identity of ethnographer by engaging in the social practices of observing, writing fieldnotes, asking questions, recording events, and discussing their findings with others. (Figure 6.5 shows a 7th-grader as Ethnographer of the Day.)

ETHNOGRAPHER OF THE DAY

Besides interviewing, another way teachers can use ethnography in the classroom is to introduce the practice of "Ethnographer of the Day." This idea began with teachers in the South Coast Writing Project led by Sheridan Blau during their summer institute. One person each day recorded notes for a "log" that would be explained the next day. This was a way of keeping track of what had happened during the institute. When my colleague, Robert Land, and I started a National Writing Project site at Cal State LA (Los Angeles Writing Project [LAWP]), we instituted the same practice and asked the fellows to take notes ethnographically. As we explained the tenets of ethnography, we asked each fellow to take descriptive notes each day and report out the next day on what they had discovered. Figure 6.2 shows the guidelines given to LAWP fellows.

FIGURE 6.2. Guidelines for LAWP Ethnographer of the Day

The Ethnographer of the Day is in charge of the Field Note Booklet for one day. The ethnographer's question is "What's going on here?" It's up to you how you make the entries and observations for your day, and any way you choose to observe and record is your choice. However, try to collect as much of the talk as possible.

Some questions to ask yourself to guide your observation:

- From whose perspective will I view this life? Mine as an insider? The director's or co-director's? The fellows'? An individual fellow's? A visitor's as an outsider?
- What events are occurring? When did the event(s) begin and when will it or they end?
- Record the language (verbatim talk) and actions.
- What roles do the participants take up? What kinds of relationships are formed?
- What are the patterns of everyday living? What are changes in the patterns? What are expected patterns?
- What must members do to be considered members? How do you know which are the members and which are the visitors?

Reporting Out. The day after you complete your observation, you will be given 10 minutes to report out on what you observed. In order to do this, analyze and reflect on your fieldnotes to answer the ethnographic questions. You might want to choose a particular event to discuss or use another audio or visual medium. You may want to have the fellows interact with you by beginning a discussion of what happened the day before. Remember, you are trying to answer the question "What's going on here?" Also, provide evidence for your interpretations.

The fellows became adept at taking fieldnotes of the activities during LAWP's Summer Institute. Reporting out the next day offered them a range of genres to use, and we soon had poems, songs, and news reports to explain what had happened the day before. The "bed-to-bed" (Graves, 1983) reports were often not received well since they were too long and detailed ("First we did this, then we did this . . ."). Instead, the fellows learned how to examine the fieldnotes they had taken and report their analysis or interpretation of the day before.

I asked them to reread their fieldnotes to discover themes or topics. These themes, or "things that strike you," have to have evidence to back up the interpretations. The evidence was found in the talk they had recorded in their fieldnotes. Often the fellows found "golden lines" spoken

FIGURE 6.3. Cathy's Ethnography Report

Cathy Cripps, Fellow from 2002 on Day 6 of the Summer Institute:

In reviewing my notes I noticed some trends, and I would like to report what trends are occurring and give some examples for each statement.

1. We are taking a little more control of this project:

    - Curtis ended up leading his own post-presentation discussion
    - Michelle was the one who asked us to "find someplace to land"
    - We decided that we needed a chart to keep track of the books
    - Some people were taking pictures
    - Some people were inquiring about the possibility of new "rooms"

2. We are becoming more comfortable with one another:

    - People are more able to object to one another's statements or opinions
    - People are more willing to say things that may cause disagreement
    - We are more willing to share very personal and emotional stories
    - There is increasing laughter (I tried to count the laughing but gave up)
    - Someone mentioned dreading our last day

3. There is some evidence that we may even be protecting each other:

    - Closing the door during Veronica's reading
    - Getting Kleenex for each other
    - Reading for each other

4. Golden lines:

    - "Whenever somebody writes about someone else, they're not. They're writing about themselves."
    - "I don't think the answers are in books as much as they are within us."
    - "Can I eat your chocolate since you're not having any?"
    - "The teacher is the buffer between the bureaucracy of the state and the kids."
    - "I don't think it brings us down. I think it brings us closer together."

by other fellows in the institute. Our writing project identified "golden lines" as special or unusual sentences spoken during the institute. Two examples of reports from LAWP ethnographers of the day are shown in Figures 6.3 and 6.4.

These two fellows from two different summer institutes analyzed their fieldnotes and discovered different themes or trends. In reporting out the next day what they found, Cathy and Peter both focused on topics that interested them. They interpreted their fieldnotes from their own perspectives as participants of the institute, and then gave evidence for those interpretations.

Cathy (Figure 6.3) found that the fellows were beginning to lead the institute, that the fellows were getting to know one another, and that the fellows were protective of one another. Peter's analysis (Figure 6.4) was in the form of contrasting pairs. He identified them as "External vs. Internal, Outsider vs. Insider, and Emergent Norms vs. Established Practices." Cathy ended her report with "golden lines." We often would put these golden lines up on the board and reflect on them.

Fly on the Wall

When the LAWP fellows went back into their classrooms in the fall, some continued Ethnographer of the Day with their students. As students learn about ethnography they learn to see classroom life from another perspective, one that views the life of the classroom from a stranger's perspective. The following example is taken from one 7th-grader's ethnographer report and illustrates how this teacher was successful in teaching his students how to look from an outsider's perspective.

Ethnography Report: *Fly on The Wall* by Selena

As you probably have gathered from the title, I am merely a fly. And, alas, having compound eyes and feet made for gripping ceilings, I can neither read nor write. Fortunately, a kind human named Selena has allowed me to dictate into her ear while she writes what I am saying. Here, then, is the classroom according to me.

Inside there were rows of desks with chairs attached and little spaces for pencils. I marveled at how everything was so organized. (Being a fly, I am naturally untidy.) But the children's attention was drawn immediately to a table at the far side of the room. Flying overhead, I could see what the students were making a mad dash for: composition books, painted in a dazzling array of colors.

I stared at the many notebooks lying on the desks. One girl had splattered her notebook with paint, quite like Jackson Pollock. Another girl had painted hers simply with a calming combination of blue and purple. Another boy's proclaimed loudly, "ANDREW WAS HERE."

Students in this 7th-grade class were coming to understand this concept of making the familiar strange, through ethnography. Selena wrote her fieldnotes from the perspective of a fly on the wall, observing the classroom as a stranger but through the voice of a participant in the class, thus,

FIGURE 6.4. Peter's Ethnography Report

Peter Worth, Fellow from 2004 on First Week

Today's themes can be classified into seemingly contrasting pairs:

1. External vs. Internal: Overall today, we (the fellows) demonstrated a politeness and willingness to try activities and participate in discussions, but later discussions revealed that much of this was done with a critical eye.

External

- We all wrote in journals or in quick-writes when asked.
- We listened silently for 31 minutes during guest's presentation before asking a question.
- We quickly jumped-in to participate as readers.

Internal

- During our debriefing session, several concerns were raised about relevance to the classroom and overall coherence of the workshop.
- Responses shared showed a deep consideration of the topics. "Don't ask a question unless you want to hear a lot of responses."

2. Outsider vs. Insider Behavior: Our behavior changes depending on whether or not we have a visitor.

Insiders

- Among insiders, conversation flows.
- People take initiative to form writing group seats. "Am I encroaching on your space?"
- During the breaks for discussion, we are committed and supportive.
- We describe ourselves as relaxed; passionate; committed; a bit off; tolerant.

Outsiders

- With outsiders, we are compliant and polite. Most people remained seated throughout the presentations and did not take breaks.
- We are proud of our group, quickly providing descriptors for the guest and telling him, "The standard introduction or bio may not cut it (with this group)."

3. Emergent Norms vs. Established Practices: As norms for the group begin to emerge naturally, we are receiving guidance on established practices of the Writing Project.

- Fellows ask for clear guidelines and expectations, such as the duties of the ethnographer and writing groups.
- Presenter and directors encourage and discourage behavior through stories and examples of previous projects.

The woman who shared the sexually explicit story with the group
The man who harshly critiques the very personal piece of writing
"What tends to happen is by about the third day . . ."

the fieldnotes reflect an outsider's view of insider activity. The traditional ethnographic term for this is *participant observer* (Spradley, 1980).

Participant Observer

When undertaking an ethnographic study, the ethnographer is the outsider who is joining the community to investigate and research the culture. The ethnographer is called a participant observer. Some anthropologists take years to learn the language of the culture they are studying. They live with the members for a certain amount of time in order to understand what it means to be part of the community. However, the ethnographer is never truly a "member" of the culture and eventually steps out of his or her initial role to report the findings.

The concept of Ethnographer of the Day brings a new definition to the meaning of participant observer. Instead of having an ethnographer enter from outside and study the culture for the whole time, the Ethnographer of the Day is already a member of the culture. He or she becomes the researcher for only 1 day. The community is examined through the eyes of one of the participants. More participants than an observers, these members get only a taste of being an ethnographer but understand more completely than a real outsider what happens in the community. This is illustrated to a greater extent in one LAWP fellow's 5th-grade classroom when she decided to teach her students about ethnography. Here is the report from one of her 5th-grade ethnographers of the day:

> Only two aliens lived and now watch over the world. Their names were Savage and Dart. The year is now 2002 where Savage and Dart chose to look over Ms. Arroyo's class in the fifth grade of Smith Elementary School. "Dart, I want you to scan the whole class to get information on them." "Right away captain. I assume you'll be watching them right?" "Yes, we need to study their moves so that one day we can make peace with each other."

The student proceeded to document the whole day as ethnographer. At the end of this four-page account the student ended the log:

> Back in space where the aliens were, "Captain Savage, how will we make peace, if all the humans do totally weird things like this class?" "I don't know Dart, I just don't know." (Frank, Arroyo, & Land, 2004, p. 373)

This piece illustrates a central point about ethnography. Ethnographers often strive to make the strange into the familiar (Spindler & Spindler, 1982). For example, when anthropologists investigate cultures in other lands, they try to describe these cultures so that they are understandable, without denigrating or devaluing those cultures in any way. However, when educational ethnographers who are born in the United States enter classrooms in the United States, they are presented with cultures that are very familiar. The goal then becomes making the familiar into the strange in order to systematically understand and analyze what is happening.

The narrative about Savage and Dart illustrates how students may come to understand the concept of making the familiar strange. The student wrote the fieldnotes in the context of aliens coming from outer space and observing the classroom as strangers and not as students. In this way the fieldnotes reflect an outsider's view of insider activity. The aliens found the events "weird," or strange. Additionally, the fieldnotes point to how ethnography can provide opportunities for a student to use his or her own particular voice when writing up and reporting out the research to communicate in different ways.

Observing from Multiple Perspectives

The students in the 5th-grade classroom above were learning how to become researchers when they took a stance as an outsider, looking from the perspective of someone who was not usually a member of the classroom. For example, one entry from a student who described the actions of a substitute teacher illustrates why observing from a different point of view can be valuable. An observation of a substitute is an ideal situation for an ethnographer because of the change in patterns, or "clash," that this offers the observer (Agar, 1994). Instead of routine patterns that are enacted day after day (and often invisible to the observer because they have not been present every day), the substitute offers the observer the chance to see how the patterns are changed, thereby making the normal patterns and practices more visible. A student named Tyler wrote in his fieldnotes:

> Every time the sub saw a person raise his/her hand, she would say thank you for raising your hand! I thought it was funny. . . . Whenever someone got the answer right, the sub would say "Gooood!" . . . I think this day is weird because everybody is talking so much. I noticed that the sub went to her desk. I guess that she went to get the homework. She said that the homework is due June 10th which is on Monday. Me and Weston smiled at each other because the homework was due on Friday. (Frank, Arroyo, & Land, 2004)

This student was able to see the differences between the normal patterns of classroom life and the changed patterns because there was a new teacher in the room. A substitute is a stranger in the room, who does not know the routines, and will make events happen differently and talk in different ways. This realization helped the ethnographer look at the classroom and see that "this day is weird because everybody is talking so much." It may be that the classroom was noisier than normal because of the substitute or it may be that the ethnographer never noticed the noise before. However, the student succeeded in becoming an outsider, if only for a moment, and was able to view life from that perspective and observe the norms and expectations of life in this particular classroom. The more that the teacher and her students used ethnography, the more they learned about emic (insider) and etic (outsider) perspectives, helping them understand how multiple perspectives add to our awareness of our own cultures.

Not only was Tyler beginning to wonder why people act and talk as they do, he was beginning to use quotations ("Gooood!"). Verbatim talk is important for ethnographers when taking fieldnotes. Many beginners write about the talk instead of writing down the words exactly as they are said (Hammersley & Atkinson, 1983). Writing about what is said instead of writing the talk verbatim is another way that the observer's interpretation creeps into the fieldnotes without his or her awareness. When we write about the talk, it becomes the researcher's perspective on what was said and not the participants' perspective. The actual talk allows the researcher to get closer to the members themselves and understand what life is like from their point of view. For example, students in this 5th grade were gathering evidence in the form of quotations for their interpretations of the reasons behind the actions of others. One student began his entry this way: "We started the day by doing the DOL [Daily Oral Language]. I noticed Chao, Mike, and Adriana were talking. Probably about tickets because Shan kept on saying, 'Dang Crazy. You have a lot.' Then Bob said, 'We should go to P.E.'" (Frank, Arroyo, & Land, 2004, p. 374)

By using the talk of other students as evidence for his interpretations of their actions, this student was engaging in one of the most important practices of ethnographers, that of speaking from evidence and not from personal opinion. He noticed that students were gathered together and talking and, then, made the hypothesis that they were talking about tickets or rewards. His evidence was the quote he overheard and wrote in his fieldnotes. In this way the research not only helped students see reasons behind the actions of others, it also helped them base their thinking and writing on evidence they had collected through observation and listening. They were taking action from informed stances as ethnographers and researchers.

These 5th-grade students had opportunities to see their school and its culture from multiple perspectives as different points of view were presented.

HOW STUDENT ETHNOGRAPHY HELPS TEACHERS

One 5th-grade student, who was a recent immigrant from Mexico, used his primary language to record the events of the day (*Cuando entramos a la clase escribimos el D.O.L.* [When we entered the class we wrote the Daily Oral Language.]). The teacher reflected on what that meant to the rest of the class:

> The student who spoke no English and did his ethnographies in Spanish also shared his ethnography the next day verbally. He would read a couple of sentences in Spanish and I would translate for the class. I think this really helped to bring out his voice and role in the class as well. The other students were forced to see things from his perspective. Occasionally he would miss something that happened that was regarded as important. This helped me to shape his instruction. Other times he misunderstood. Many times he saw something that no one else saw and the other students, many of whom didn't speak Spanish, were fascinated. (Mary Eileen, as quoted in Frank, Arroyo, & Land, 2004)

In this instance, the 5th-grade teacher discovered that having her students become ethnographers gave her another resource for understanding the lives of her students at school. Their fieldnotes gave her insight into their own 10-year-old perspectives, especially regarding how time was used and how much homework they had. In fieldnotes, students described how their school day was structured according to the different classes they attended and noted that "first we did this and then we did that." Scheduling was an important consideration in the students' lives as they were hurled from one discipline to another, not because of student interests or teacher ideas about learning, but due to the institutional demands of time management. During a health class, one Ethnographer of the Day documented how a discussion about foods was cut short. His fieldnotes illustrate that the discussion was terminated when he looked at the clock:

> They all said, Are all foods the same? When we were done Parker asked, will eating watermelon and then drinking water make your

stomach hurt. Mrs. D answered him, I don't know then Parker said
I'll try it and told her that he was going to do that then I looked
at the clock and it was time to go so we all went to writing class.
(student quoted in Frank, Arroyo, & Land, 2004, p. 374)

Student interests of the moment did not determine activities but rather they had to engage in instruction on the basis of a preset schedule. The fieldnotes illustrated how students were rushed from one topic to another without time to connect or reflect on their learning. Just as they became interested in one concept they were shifted to another period.

Another insight the teacher gained from looking through the students' ethnography reports was that the accounts for each day usually referred to homework. The students at this urban school switched classes for mathematics, writing, science, English Language Development (ELD), and social studies. In January, one student described the amount of homework students received:

At 8:35 it was time for ELD. We went to the teacher's desk to play
a game while Miss Arroyo checked our *homework*. After the game
we did a Spelling Test. At 9:15 we went to math and corrected our
homework. Then the substitute told us our *homework*. I was done
with mine. At 10:50 we went to recess. I played four corners. At
10:15 we went to science class. We had to turn in our *homework*.
Then we looked at animal cells. Then for our *homework*, we had
to draw an animal cell. At 11:05 we went to writing class. We did
our journal and turned in our *homework*. (student quoted in Frank,
Arroyo, & Land, 2004, p. 375)

In self-contained elementary classrooms, one teacher usually assigns the homework. However, as these 5th-grade students illustrated, homework was assigned by many teachers and became a major component in their lives as students. Homework was a repeated pattern in their culture.

SUMMARY

When students become ethnographers and observe what's going on in school, the events of their academic lives take on more meaning. They notice more and reflect back on their experiences and record their community life. They have opportunities to observe classrooms and academic content from an outside perspective. Students assume the identity of ethnographers by engaging in the social practices of observing,

FIGURE 6.5. Reporting Out as Ethnographer of the Day

writing fieldnotes, asking questions, recording events, and discussing their findings with others. In this way, they become researchers of their own learning and may begin to ask questions about what is being taught and why. (Figure 6.5 shows a 7th-grade Ethnographer of the Day presenting his observations from the day before.)

Activities to Explore the Ideas

1. Interview a teacher who is using ethnography in the classroom. Use your skills as an interviewer to discover as much information as you can.
2. Interview the children in a classroom using ethnography. Remember the ideas presented in Chapter 4 as you investigate ethnography from their perspective.

Suggested Readings

Egan-Robertson, A., & Bloome, D. (Eds.). (1998). *Students as researchers of culture and language in their own communities*. Cresskill, NJ: Hampton Press.

This book gives teachers many ideas for initiating ethnography in the classroom with students. Two especially noteworthy chapters in the book are "Learning to Write by Writing Ethnography," by Toby Curry and David Bloome, and "Learning to See Learning in the Classroom: Developing an Ethnographic Perspective," by Beth Yeager, Ana Floriani, and Judith Green.

CHAPTER 7

Conclusion

Doing ethnography always leads to a profound awareness that
a particular cultural meaning system is almost inexhaustibly rich.
(Spradley, 1979, p. 204)

I began this book with three questions: (1) How do ethnographic interviews help teachers learn more about students and parents? (2) How do ethnographic interviews help preservice teachers explore the work of their mentor teachers? and (3) How can teachers use ethnography with students as a resource for learning about the world?

TEACHERS AND CHILDREN, TEACHERS AND PARENTS

The goal of ethnographic interviews is to gain information, to discover— to find out about the life of the informant. When teachers interview children or parents they cross cultural boundaries by letting go of their own particular biases and look instead from the perspective of the child or parent. Seeing the world from another's perspective is the beginning of understanding multiple perspectives. Investigating another's perspective is a way of adding information. Looking at all the different perspectives gives the most information available. And how many other perspectives have we not even thought of? What about interviewing friends or siblings of the child?

Thoughtful conversations between teachers and children and between teachers and parents enhance relationships. Teachers learn about families and neighborhoods where their students live and play. These relationships have the power to bridge the gap between home and school. Teachers discover the special talents of children and parents in order to guide instruction. Drawing on this knowledge, teachers can recommend resources to enhance children's learning.

ETHNOGRAPHY AND PRESERVICE TEACHERS

By providing a systematic approach to observation and interviewing, ethnographic methods enhance novice teachers' understanding of the culture of teaching. Instead of approaching teaching from their own personal memories of how their teachers taught them, beginning teachers use ethnography to tap into the master teacher's decision making. They begin to learn the language of teaching and are able to communicate and question experienced teachers.

Instead of interpreting classroom observations from their own personal perspectives, ethnography teaches novice teachers to hold off on making judgments until evidence has been accumulated. Preservice teachers learn to observe and interview in order to understand the classroom from the teacher's perspective. What are the goals she or he has in mind? What is the teacher trying to accomplish? What kind of planning did the teacher do to set up this classroom or this lesson? What did the teacher think about? Answering these questions with evidence from observations and interviews instead of making assumptions is the work of ethnographers.

ETHNOGRAPHY IN THE CLASSROOM

Instead of assigning pages in the social studies or science text, teachers are using the research tools of ethnography to assist children in learning about the world. The special interests of the children are paramount in developing questions and collecting data. Teaching children how to develop questions is part of schooling. It's about teaching children to be critical learners who notice the world and the people and places in it.

Observing and interviewing offer children a chance to collect their own information instead of having it handed to them in a textbook. Children learn how to categorize and organize the information they collect. They compare and contrast different viewpoints, taking information from all perspectives. Reflecting on the final data collection and writing up the reports strengthens children's awareness of the importance of communicating the outcome.

HOME VISITS

Home visits will not be as difficult for teachers who are already in classrooms as it is for preservice teachers who don't yet have connections.

Meeting parents at open house and parent conferences allows the teacher to gain entry to the family. When they gain access to the home for visits, ethnography teaches them how to listen and talk less and to ask questions about the child and the family and not about school. Learning to interview by surrendering the outcome to the informant, being still and not jumping to judgments, repeating and probing for more information, and sitting down and eating with the parents are all good ways to begin to know the whole child.

Teachers are sometimes criticized for being authoritarian about school, and are accused of thinking they know more or better than parents do. Teachers do know more about teaching and learning than most parents. They have spent long hours in classes learning instructional strategies, assessment procedures, and teaching activities. But the criticism is valid when it comes to the home and family. We need to forge the connection between school and home since education is better when teachers and parents work together.

As the interviews in this book have shown, many immigrant populations do not have access to schools where home visits are the norm. Living in poor communities—sometimes unsafe communities—makes it more difficult for families and teachers to connect. But as the cases presented in this book have illustrated, it is not impossible to make home visits in urban communities. It has to be a commitment that teachers and parents take on and realize is just as important as good books or access to technology. Parents and teachers need to know each other if the child is to get the best education possible.

References

Agar, M. (1980). *The professional stranger: An informal introduction to ethnography.* New York: Academic Press.

Agar, M. (1994). *Language shock: Understanding the culture of conversation.* New York: William Morrow.

Allard, H., & Marshall, J. (1977). *Miss Nelson is missing.* New York: Scholastic.

Atwell, N. (1987). *In the middle: Writing, reading, and learning with adolescents.* Portsmouth, NH: Heinemann.

Calkins, L. M. (1986). *The art of teaching writing.* Portsmouth, NH: Heinemann.

Cazden, C. B. (2001). *Classroom discourse: The language of teaching and learning.* Portsmouth, NH: Heinemann.

Cook-Gumperz, J., & Gumperz, J. J. (1981). From oral to written culture: The transition to literacy. In M. Whiteman (Ed.), *Variations in writing: Functional and linguistic-cultural difference* (pp. 13–23). Hillsdale, NJ: Erlbaum.

Corsaro, W. (1981). Entering the child's world: Research strategies for field entry and data collection in a preschool setting. In J. Green & C. Wallat (Eds.), *Ethnography and language in educational settings* (pp. 117–146). Norwood, NJ: Ablex.

Curry, T., & Bloome, D. (1998). Learning to write by writing ethnography. In A. Egan-Robertson & D. Bloome (Eds.), *Students as researchers of culture and language in their own communities* (pp. 37–58). Cresskill, NJ: Hampton Press.

Dixon, C. N., Frank, C. R., & Green, J. L. (1999). Classroom as cultures: Toward understanding the constructed nature of life in classrooms. *Primary Voices K–6, 7*(3), 4–8.

Edwards, A. D., & Westgate, D. P. G. (1994). *Investigating classroom talk* (2nd ed.). London: Falmer.

Egan-Robertson, A., & Bloome, D. (Eds.). (1998). *Students as researchers of culture and language in their own communities.* Cresskill, NJ: Hampton Press.

Erickson, F. (1982). Classroom discourse as improvisation: Relationships between academic task structure and social participation in lessons. In L. C. Wilkinson (Ed.), *Communicating in the classroom* (pp. 153–182). New York: Academic Press.

Frank, C., Arroyo, M., & Land, R. (2004). The ethnography book. *Language Arts, 81*(5), 368–376.

Frank, C. R. (1999). *Ethnographic eyes: A teacher's guide to classroom observation.* Portsmouth, NH: Heinemann.

Frank, C. R., & Uy, F. L. (2004). Ethnography for teacher education. *Journal of Teacher Education, 55*(3), 269–283.

Gee, J. (1985). The narrativization of experience in the oral style. *Journal of Education,167*(1), 9–35.

Geertz, C. (1973). *The interpretation of cultures.* New York: Basic Books.

Goody, E. (1978). *Questions and politeness.* Cambridge, United Kingdom: Cambridge University Press.

Graves, D. H. (1983). *Writing: Teachers and children at work.* Exeter, NH: Heinemann.

Green, J. L. (1992). Multiple perspectives: Issues and directions. In R. Beach, J. L. Green, M. L. Kamil, & T. Shanahan (Eds.), *Multidisciplinary perspectives on literacy research* (pp. 19–33). Urbana, IL: National Council of Teachers of English.

Green, J. L., & Bloome, D. (1997). Ethnography and ethnographers of and in education: A situated perspective. In S. B. Heath, J. Flood, & D. Lapp (Eds.), *Handbook for research in the communicative and visual arts* (pp. 181–202). New York: Macmillan.

Gumperz, J. J. (1986). Interactional sociolinguistics on the study of schooling. In J. Cook-Gumperz (Ed.), *The social construction of literacy* (pp. 45–68). New York: Cambridge University Press.

Hammersley, M., & Atkinson, P. (1983). *Ethnography: Principles in practice.* London: Tavistock.

Heath, S. B. (1983). *Ways with words: Language, life and work in communities and classrooms.* Cambridge, UK: Cambridge University Press.

Mishler, E. G. (1986). *Research interviewing: Context and narrative.* Cambridge, MA: Harvard University Press.

Modarres, A. (2010). The CSU is "the place for promise" for countless Californians: An examination of academic cuts and changes reflecting on Cal State Los Angeles. *California Faculty,* (2), 21–25.

Posnick-Goodwin, S. (2002, February). Home visits attempt to strengthen connection between parents and schools. *California Educator, 6*(5), 20–22.

Posnick-Goodwin, S. (2007, February). Home visit projects have the potential to reinvigorate teachers, involve parents. *California Educator, 11*(5), 26–27.

Putney, L., & Frank, C. (2008). Looking through ethnographic eyes at classrooms acting as cultures. *Ethnography and Education, 3*(2), 211–228.

Spindler, G., & Spindler, L. (1982). Roger Harker and Schonhausen: From familiar to strange and back again. In G. Spindler (Ed.), *Doing the ethnography of schooling: Educational anthropology in action* (pp. 20–46). Prospect Heights, Il: Waveland Press.

Spradley, J. P. (1979). *The ethnographic interview.* New York: Harcourt Brace Jovanovich.

Spradley, J. P. (1980). *Participant observation.* San Francisco: Holt, Rinehart & Winston.

Spradley, J. P., & McCurdy, D. W. (1972). *The cultural experience: Ethnography in complex society.* Prospect Heights, IL: Waveland Press.

Tammivaara, J., & Enright, D. S. (1986). On eliciting information: Dialogues with child informants. *Anthropology & Education Quarterly, 17*(4), 218–238.

Weade, R., & Green, J. L. (1989). Reading in the instructional context: An interactional sociolinguistic/ethnographic perspective. In C. Emihovich (Ed.), *Locating learning: Ethnographic perspectives on classroom research* (pp. 17–56). Norwood, NJ: Ablex.

Yeager, B. (1999). Constructing a community of inquirers. *Primary Voices K–6, 7*(3), 37–52.

Yeager, B., Floriani, A., & Green, J. (1998). Learning to see learning in the classroom: Developing an ethnographic perspective. In A. Egan-Robertson & D. Bloome (Eds.), *Students as researchers of culture and language in their own communities* (pp. 115–140). Cresskill, NJ: Hampton Press.

Index

About the Author

Carolyn Frank is a professor in the Charter College of Education and the director of the Los Angeles Writing Project, both at California State University, Los Angeles. Her research interests focus on the classrooms of writing project teachers using ethnographic methods of observation and interviewing.